TEX SIMONE:
THE MAN WHO SAVED
BASEBALL IN SYRACUSE

By

William Humber, John Simone, and Wendy Simone Shoen

Published by:
Wildebeest Publishing Company, LLC
Syracuse, New York

Do you have a story to tell? What's your animal spirit? Share it with us. #hellobeesties

You may visit the authors websites at www.texsimone.com

Wildebeest Publishing Co.

Wildebeest Publishing Company, LLC

For more information about copyrights and usage, special discounts on bulk purchases, workshops, and engagements, please contact Wildebeest Publishing Company, LLC at (315) 220-0217, info@wildebeestpublishing.com, or online at www.wildebeestpublishing.com

Wildebeest Publishing is dedicated to providing flexible remote work opportunities and has a presence in Syracuse, New York City, Denver, and Tampa.

Wildebeest Publishing Company, LLC paperback First Edition September 2024, United States of America

Photographs property of The Simone Family
Cover Photo Credit: The Post-Standard | Syracuse.com | Nichols Lisi, Staff Photographer

ISBN 978-1-958233-32-0
LLCN 2024918609

Daddy, we always talked about writing a book.
You were our treasure, and your life was one
to be remembered and told.
Our love for you will live on forever.
—Always, your daughter, Wendy

TABLE OF CONTENTS

FOREWORD

Paul Beeston, President and later President Emeritus, Toronto Blue Jays baseball Club

It's safe to say Tex Simone **was** the Syracuse Chiefs. For instance, our success (the Toronto Blue Jays) wouldn't have been possible without Tex. We first met around 1978 when we signed the working relationship with Syracuse as our Triple-A affiliate. Though community-owned and operated, they had a direct affiliation with a major league team, the Blue Jays, through the standardized Player Development Contract or PDC.

Tex perfectly understood the role of a Minor League team: to develop players for the majors. For a new expansion team like ours, that was particularly important. We didn't always give him a playoff team. We'd send players to him who weren't necessarily Triple-A ready, and, on the other hand, Bobby Mattick would be pushing guys like a Dave Stieb up to the Majors. In 1985, Tom Henke left them in July even though the Chiefs were in a pennant chase because we needed him in Toronto. Tex never complained.

He got the big picture. He realized the importance of building relationships, not only with us but also with his managers, coaches, trainers, and the community. He knew we were his stakeholders; with everyone it was always professional, always courteous. It's what baseball is or should be about. And keep in mind he had to answer to shareholders for what was then a community-owned team.

On the other hand, he was always aware of the bottom line. He never overspent. I think he'd re-string a ball if he knew how to do it. When he came up to Toronto or down to Dunedin, he'd always go away with a couple dozen balls for use in batting practice for the Chiefs. He treated people the way they wanted to be treated. He wasn't a drinker, and he even gave up smoking, which he had enjoyed with a cup of coffee. Despite all of his medical challenges, he never changed. After I left the Jays, I'd see less of him, maybe once a year, but when we did run into each other, we'd pick up where we'd left off, just as if we'd seen each other the day before.

There are people who mean something to the Blue Jays, who were critical to our success. He was one of them. He was a baseball lifer, and he knew where he wanted to be. He never aspired to the majors. He knew he had the right job in the right place. He had all he needed; it was a life blessed with richness. Under Tex, the Chiefs were a family operation, and when you went there, you felt like you were part of that family. Likewise, even though they weren't on our payroll, we always made them feel welcome in Toronto or Dunedin.

He was instrumental in our success, and that meant so much because relationships between major and minor league teams aren't always easy. I was always welcomed when I went to Syracuse. Tex occasionally gave me his honest and occasionally critical observations on the relationship, but they were never demands. He had your back even though he couldn't always win with what we gave him. Two words describe Tex – "The Gentleman."

Ariel Shoen-Ornstein, Granddaughter
of Anthony Tex Simone

When my grandfather passed in March of 2015, people from all facets of his community shared memories of his life with us that brought much-needed comfort in a time of deep and immense grief. Stories I'd never heard and people I'd never met had somehow managed to bring all of us a smile, a laugh, a moment of peace. In the months following, I regretted not having asked my grandfather more questions about his childhood, his time in the military, and the early days of his baseball career. We had an unbelievably special bond that gave us the gift of precious time together throughout my entire life, and because of that, I probably knew more than most grandchildren did about their grandfather. But I had always wished for more. I enjoyed hearing the incredible baseball stories he would share of his first-ever spring training in St. Petersburg, Florida, rubbing shoulders and sharing lockers with some of baseball's all-time greats. I enjoyed hearing about the struggles of saving baseball in Syracuse and how he was able to succeed. It was because of these stories from my grandfather that I chose my own career in sports and carry on his legacy every single day.

I'd like to think of this book as just that – a continuation of his legacy. Not only as a distinguished baseball executive but, more importantly, as the human that he was and the life that he lived. The human with a heart for others in every area of his life – his family, his friends, his fellow parishioners at church, the countless charities he was so passionate about, the players from his 54 years in baseball and their families, the list goes on. He was a young boy raised on the North Side of Syracuse by Italian immigrant parents who would go on to become a talented young high school athlete, a sergeant in the United States Army, a businessman, a groundskeeper, a trainer, a general manager, an Executive Vice President, and a CEO. Someone who truly lived the American dream and worked his way from the very bottom to the very top.

I'm so grateful that my uncle has the memory of an elephant and remembers so many of the stories my grandfather shared in such detail. Thanks to him and my mom's knack for hanging on to keepsakes, we were able to compile some of these incredible stories into this book to share with everyone.

A special thanks to Bill Humber for helping us put it all together in a way that made sense and for taking the time to talk to people near and dear to my grandfather and listen to the stories we remembered that shaped his life.

INTRODUCTION

21 August 1928 – 6 March 2015

Anthony "Tex" Simone was a man for all seasons. Spring was the return of baseball, summer its ultimate flowering, fall a time of postseason invitations, and winter his attendance at the sport's annual meetings and laying the groundwork for the coming season. Baseball was central to Tex Simone's life. A public trust had been invested in him, and it was one he honored and then enhanced. It kept baseball alive and flourishing in Syracuse, New York. His days spanned the time shortly after the Los Angeles Dodgers essentially gave the storied Montreal Royals franchise away for $35,000 to a few years before its eventual sale to the New York Mets for $18 million. Of equal importance, however, was his love for his family and his faith. To the end of his life, they sustained his well-being through the challenges brought on by aging.

Minor League Baseball, regardless of its level or connection to a major league lifeline, is a realm of paradox in which you want to win but know that the means to do so may be snatched away at the most crucial time of the year. Where once a quasi-independence reigned in which aging veterans filled out a roster with promising youth, today's minor league entity is a pure function of its major league affiliate's needs for player development and call-up when necessary. As such, the chief role of the minor league proprietor is to ensure every home game has a plethora of sound, activity, and special treats only marginally connected to the performance of the two teams on the field.

Tex's baseball journey began as an unpaid volunteer preparing the field before game time, to trainer, general manager, and, eventually, senior Vice President with a street named in his honor and a marble bust featuring a prominent Roman nose, a salute to his Italian heritage. Opportunities for big league ascension came his way over the years, but his commitment was to a city whose prosperous days were behind it as it transitioned into one content with a mid-level place alongside larger, more successful American cities. Those years were not always kind to his hometown as he watched the decline of the world he grew up in, most notably his precious Little Italy of prosperous restaurants and shops. Problematic social and economic issues traumatized many cities like Syracuse.

A lesser man might have thrown in the towel rather than await a renewed golden age, particularly after a disastrous fire wiped out the ballpark's central seating area in 1969. Instead, it only reinforced the commitment of Tex and his family in ensuring the Syracuse Chiefs remained and prospered. Eventually, there would be a new stadium in 1997, but regardless of the apparent prosperity, Tex always realized dark days might follow. It became a running joke among family members that no ball was too imperfect that it couldn't be used again. The hunt for lost baseballs occupied many pre-game rituals. In this and other ways, he engaged his entire family, from his wife Joanne, his son and daughter John and Wendy, and eventually his grandchildren, in all aspects of the team's operation, paying them at rates far below market value. It often brought unfair claims of nepotism, but it saved the team's bottom line and its future on a continual basis. His grandson Adam recalls, "I remember when I was younger, around five or six, I used to pick up garbage with my brother Andrew in the parking lot, and I always used to find money. I found out later that my grandpa used to find out where I was going and put money there."

It is a somewhat bitter pill that the salvation job he performed eventually brought millions of dollars in profit for others when the New York Mets bought the team as their Triple-A farm team. By then, the Simones were gone from running the team, but the experience of doing so was not wasted on a younger generation of family members, many of whom have made their way into some other aspect of baseball. This is the story of how Tex did it – how, against all odds, he kept top-flight minor league baseball alive in Syracuse, contributed directly to the World Series success story of a city outside the United States, and left a legacy of respect for what a person can achieve despite uncertain prospects.

As no less than the greatest exponent of the English language, William Shakespeare wrote in Julius Caesar, Act 4, Scene 3.

> *There is a tide in the affairs of men,*
> *Which taken at the flood, leads on to fortune;*
> *Omitted, all the voyage of their life*
> *Is bound in shallows and in miseries.*
> *On such a full sea are we now afloat,*
> *And we must take the current when it serves,*
> *Or lose our ventures.*

Tex Simone rode that tide and it led to a greater fortune, the maintenance and future security of what he had assumed as a public trust. It was a function of a love of baseball and his devout faith, which, in his later years, he was so well-respected by the Nuns they invited him in to pray with them, an honor rarely given to others. His nickname, Tex, made it onto the cemetery wall plaque, marking his final resting place. His name is renowned in the city and throughout baseball and has inspired younger generations of his family

His grandson Alexander now lives in Austin, Texas and has trained many professional and amateur baseball players and often runs into someone who knew his grandfather. From scouts he met coaching in the Cape Cod League to former players and managers he meets on a daily basis, they all ask, "Are you Tex Simone's grandson?"

Today, his granddaughter Ariel works with baseball players to sort out their logistical requirements beyond the ballpark, everything from setting up their home in a new city to assisting in their day-to-day needs. Most have no idea who Tex was, but there are others like veterans who are performing functions for the New York Yankees, such as Ron Guidry. It's been almost 50 years since he played in Syracuse, but when Ariel was tasked with setting up his Spring Training housing in 2023 and met him on move-in day, telling him who her grandfather was, his eyes lit up, and he joyously recalled what the man meant for him, "He treated us like we were part of his family." There could not be a more wonderful eulogy for this man for all seasons.

Today

The Syracuse Chiefs have passed out of the personal and business stewardship of the Simone family, specifically son John, who had become the team's General Manager in 1996, and daughter Wendy Shoen, described as the quiet one behind the scenes who did everything from answering phones to sewing ripped uniforms to directing merchandise sales. Nor is it any longer a community-owned entity. It has even foregone its long-historic nickname of the Chiefs in favor of that of its new owner, the Mets. In the end, the family's long-time role could not overcome the rivalries, jealousies, and critical perspectives of others, but most predominantly, the rapidly increasing value of Triple-A franchises. This factor made them prime take-over targets, particularly if their ownership model was under-financed.

Community-owned teams face significant challenges keeping their head above water if financial losses mount. Their ability to do so in Syracuse for so many years was, at first, thanks to the often unseen generosity of community benefactors, like one-time Syracuse Mayor and banker Tony Henninger. This was followed by a family-like relationship with their affiliate, the Toronto Blue Jays. Ultimately, it was due to the sacrifices, imagination, and dogged determination of Anthony "Tex" Simone. He volunteered his own family, often at significantly below market pay, to assume many of the daily functions of a minor league baseball team.

Eventually, those financial challenges meant a new private ownership model was necessary, one capable of sustaining short-term losses but also able to dip into private sources of funding not available to a publicly owned entity with so many community shareholders. There are unhappy matters associated with the above process. Criticism could be reserved for multiple actors but, in fairness to everyone, it might only have reached a state of financial disrepair requiring external intervention because, against all odds, it had been kept alive and prospered for so many years under the leadership of Tex Simone and his family. Without that glue, the inevitable monetary realities would have taken their toll much earlier.

It is not our purpose of this book to dwell on today's Syracuse Mets. That's a story for another author attuned to the nature of baseball in its third decade of the 21st century. Our interest instead is charting the amazing success story of Tex Simone. Without his determination, there would be no baseball in Syracuse, and the fate of today's team would be moot. This is a celebration of his commitment to his city and its team and of an era in baseball increasingly seen in the sport's rearview mirror, particularly as it wrestles with contraction at the minor league level. Others can judge whether that is a good or necessary thing.

This is the story about one of baseball's true believers, for whom his love of the game was trumped only by his family and faith. However, even his beloved family had to obey one of Tex's unyielding commandments. "Their lives are governed by the baseball schedule," he once said, "For us, nothing happens from April to September. No weddings, confirmations, birthdays." The first two would seem capable of planning around, but one can't be so certain about the latter!

Syracuse, New York

Statistics tell us many things. They can hold just enough truth to explain why one thing declines while another flourishes. Still, if all of life were reduced to a binary equation telling us that "x" always inevitably leads to "y," we'd have no need for imagination, commitment, and plain hard work running against a crueler fortune. Syracuse, perched in the central region of New York State, has had many lives.

At one time, it was the exclusive home of the Haudenosaunee or the Onondaga Nation. They were part of the Iroquois Confederacy, spanning much of upstate New York. They remain claimants to tradition (which will play a role in our baseball story) and residence here, though on a greatly reduced territory.

Through the 19th and into the 20th century, Syracuse became a hardscrabble industrial working-class town in which Italian, German, Greek, Irish, African-American, and other newcomers made things – real things from farm implements, candles and bicycles to, eventually, auto parts and air conditioning systems. Gradually, this golden age of production wound down, and with it, Syracuse's population descended from a 1950 high of 220,000 to 145,000 by 2010, though this was somewhat compensated for by growth in the greater Syracuse metropolitan area.

According to the World Population Review in 2020, "City leaders were surprised to find that the population of Central New York grew by 1.4% in the last decade, hitting an all-time high of 742,000 in the four-county Syracuse area." The latter being suburban and ex-urban residents. Driving into the city or identifying with its teams may not be the attraction it once was.

As well, today's triumphant digital economy has made the prospects for places like Syracuse even more precarious as the production of many physical things in smaller places is no longer needed when they can be sent electronically from creator to customer. Fortunately, Syracuse's golden age made many other things possible, including an elite university and a mid-20th century prosperous downtown, which once again is attracting a more urban-oriented generation keen on walkability and, most significantly for our story, baseball.

THE WORLD TEX
GREW UP IN

As one of the youngest Simones, Anthony had a charmed youth despite the limitations of the 1930s. Children like him from large families had room to roam, discover, and experiment with the world around them. Parents were somewhat more relaxed, having become accustomed to the trials and errors of the child-rearing process. Nearby Schiller Park was a place for all-day ball games. "We hung out there till dark," Tex later recalled, "Our parents didn't have much money, so we didn't have cars and things. To earn some money, I sold newspapers at a downtown street corner." He never forgot the headlines following the Japanese attack on Pearl Harbor in 1941. He sold more papers that day than he had ever sold before or after.

Ironically, given the similar preferences of today's urban generation, young Anthony Simone walked everywhere. In his case, there was no other choice. Whether it was to meet his father and walk home with him from Tino's Restaurant in Little Italy. Or crossing the street to Schiller Park, where sultry summer afternoons were spent playing baseball. Or attending his family's church, Our Lady of Pompei / St. Peter, for baptisms, communions, and Sunday Mass. Or venturing downtown to see the latest cowboy flick from which his nickname of Tex derived. And finally, hiking up the hill to the Municipal Stadium where the city's ball team, the Chiefs, had welcomed Triple-A league opponents since 1934. Only a lucky few had a car; what had been a luxury in the 1920s was now even further removed from most people's reach in the decade of the Depression. So, you walked ... and walked ... and walked ... and thought nothing of it.

Tino's has long since gone, but the church remains, as does a ballpark that opened in 1997 on the nearby footprint of Municipal, later MacArthur, Stadium, and so does Schiller Park, but its game of choice today is soccer reflecting the changing demographics of Tex's old neighborhood. Across the street from where Tino's had once served generations of locals, the Columbus Bakery still turns out its daily round of exquisite, crusty breads, its ovens resembling those in the movie *Moonstruck*. One half expects the one-handed Ronny Cammareri, as played by Nicholas Cage, to make an appearance. Despite the changes, it still seems like the ghosts of Syracuse's Little Italy walk the aisles of its churches, schools, and playgrounds, either metaphorically or literally. The metaphorical ones might be the stuff of a literary world of fiction, while the literal ones belong with the unexplained, the supernormal, and until proven otherwise, a non-fiction world. Each person takes their own explanation to heart, but no one denies the power of the imagination and the legacy of the departed.

Today's neighborhood has a less-than-salutary city-wide image with support services and accommodation for the indigent and economically deprived, as well as places meeting the needs of new immigrants, some of whom crowd the recreation complex in Schiller Park as part of the city's summer outreach program for children. Perhaps one day, they will look back with fondness on their own early days here.

Baseball in Syracuse

Baseball in 19th-century Syracuse had brief flings with the major leagues in the upstart International Association of 1878, followed by a season in the National League, and later lasting one year in the National League's rival, the American Association. However, most of the city's baseball history has been amongst the elite of the game's minor league, beginning in 1886 with the Syracuse Stars.

The Syracuse Chiefs name dates back to their inaugural International League season of 1934. Soon after, young Anthony was a regular patron. It was followed by the glory days of the 1940s when they reached the Junior World Series, a best-of-seven affair pitting the Triple-A minor league playoff champions of the American Association against those of the International League. Unfortunately, they lost three times and then again in 1954. A few seasons later, Syracuse was in a lower league, the Eastern, and then the team left town.

In retrospect, the minor leagues through those years looked like places where not only the best players but also growing cities like Kansas City, Baltimore, Minneapolis, Denver, Atlanta, Toronto, and Montreal got in line for a major league opportunity. Other places were forever doomed to be the proverbial minor league lifer whose major league aspirations were seen only in a rearview mirror. Cities such as Buffalo, Rochester, and Syracuse fit the latter description.

After the departure of their Eastern League team, there was no guarantee Syracuse would ever get back into organized baseball. By the end of the 1960 season, the relocated Los Angeles Dodgers abandoned their long affiliation with the Montreal Royals dating back to the franchise's days in Brooklyn. Its future uncertain, the International League team left Canada for Syracuse. The Chiefs were reborn. The life of a young man, Anthony "Tex" Simone, was about to change irrevocably, and despite whichever of Shakepeare's "shallows and miseries" might slowly be afflicting his hometown, one sporting aspect became vibrant and life-enhancing.

STEP BACK A MOMENT

L et's step back a moment to where this story, at least partially, begins, in a small village of under 500 people at the edge of Majella National Park in the Italian province of Pescara in the country's Abruzzo region above the Adriatic Sea. Today, one can purchase a property ranging from a hundred thousand Euros to over a million or rent a villa for several hundred American dollars a night in this small village of Abbateggio.

Visitors can take advantage of services like *Home Food*, an Italian agency that protects and enhances the typical Italian gastronomic and culinary legacy by showcasing the cooking of local families and providing opportunities for tourists to be their guests. A New York Times story (6 April 2010) described one such feast consisting of spaghetti alla chitarra dressed with tomato-and-lamb ragù, along with wild boar sausage, chunky prosciutto, and a sharp pecorino courtesy of the local sheep. A wine and a coffee spiked with mountain herbs of the Abruzzo region ensured a never-to-be-forgotten evening. Such a place of epicurean delight, extraordinary scenery, and potential real property extravagance, for which some elements of the latter date back to the village's founding a thousand years ago, begs an obvious question … why would anyone leave?

While today it may be a contemporary host to affluent global visitors, it was not always so renowned or so certain its annual harvest of grain, olives, vines, and fruit trees would yield sufficient rewards for the labor of its residents. Cheese and honey produced on-site might supplement a person's needs, but there were few social supports other than the kindness of neighbors if circumstances spun out of control.

Dominic Simone was born in Abbateggio in 1889. His last name remains to this day the surname of 30% of the village's inhabitants. Life in the late 19th and early 20th century had large amounts of uncertainty, even for a man named Simone, despite so many nearby relatives, namesake cousins, and, in Dominic's case, his family's well-earned status. At age 14 in 1903, he left this future tourist paradise, jumping on a boat for the promised land of America.

Tex later recalled that his father said very little about his life in Italy or about his motivation for leaving. When Tex visited the village, he said, "We looked up the City Hall records and found out my father's dad was the city clerk, almost like the mayor. He was the only educated person in the city, and he taught my father. So, when Dad came to Syracuse, he sang in Latin in church but also while he cooked, either at Tino's Restaurant [at 425 North Salina in Syracuse's Little Italy] or at home."

One of Dominic's first jobs in America was in a canning factory. Here, he met Rose Campanella, the other person central to Tex Simone's story. She was three years younger, but her family had come from Italy ten years before Dominic. Dominic and Rose married in 1914, and a year later, their son Archie was born. Six children followed: Marie, Angeline, Nicholas, Louise, Anthony, and Dominic. Anthony was born on August 21, 1928, just a year before the devastating world depression. Home was on North Townsend Street, then Highland, and later 227 Grumbach Avenue.

In many American places, the Italian immigrants of the late 19th and early 20th century had contended with racial stereotypes all too commonly directed at recently freed African Americans. Brent Staples's New York Times article, "How Italians Became White" (13 October 2019), described how this xenophobia culminated in the New Orleans mob-incited lynching of 11 Italian immigrants in 1891 after trials had cleared many of the accused, with mistrials for others, in the murder of a popular city police chief. The government of

Italy reacted with fury breaking off diplomatic relations, demanding compensation, and suggesting war might result.

President Benjamin Harrison acquiesced to their monetary demands, promised to tackle the issue of mob violence (for everyone except Black Americans), and publicly recognized Columbus Day in 1892 as the 400th Anniversary of Genoa-born Cristoforo Colombo's successful Atlantic Ocean voyage under the flag of Spain.

For first-generation Italian-Americans everywhere, it was a time to maintain a low profile, work hard, and eventually acquire a home and raise a growing family. They had little time for fun and games, but this lack of interest was not true for their children. Sports became a central defining feature for second and later generations of Italian-Americans. From these families came many of the legends of American sports, including Joe DiMaggio, Yogi Berra, and Rocky Marciano, as well as the core of the United States soccer team from St. Louis's Italian-American neighborhood, the Hill, who stunned England 1-0 at the 1950 World Cup in Brazil. Syracuse likewise would produce a sporting legend, though one who eventually graduated from the playing field to that of management.

ANTHONY BECOMES TEX

Municipal Stadium, built under Franklin D. Roosevelt's Civil Works Administration program, opened in 1934 on what were described as "wastelands in the city's northeast corner." It was home to the city's International League baseball team, the Chiefs. A young boy could hardly ask for more, but more there was! Downtown Syracuse was a world of surprises ranging from store windows in an age before suburban shopping malls to movie theaters, the latter of which contributed to Tex Simone's unusual nickname.

How did Anthony Simone, or Tony as they called him years later in the army, the son of Italian immigrants, get a name redolent of a world featuring six-shooters, bucking broncos, and a cowboy's distinctive gait? No one is absolutely certain, but the most reliable account says it grew out of this young boy's fascination with the "oaters," or cowboy westerns, seemingly on a permanent cycle through the local neighborhood theater. They were a regular staple of 1930s Saturday afternoon entertainment for kids who paid a nickel to be entertained by Gabby Hayes, Roy Rogers, Gene Autry, and, for comic relief, Andy Devine. A buddy of Tex's was an usher, and his assistance often allowed them free entry.

According to Bob Fruciano, "He got the nickname after we came out of a Tex Ritter film, and we all played the role of characters out of the old west. He drew his make-believe gun and dropped the whole bunch of us in the middle of the sidewalk. We hung the nickname Tex on him, never thinking it would stick." Stick it did. By the time high school rolled around for Tex and his friends in the early 1940s, their freewheeling days and playground adventures had primed them for athletic excellence in a forum extensively reported in the media of the day. As a result, Tex Simone's basketball, baseball, and football prowess at North High and beyond were known throughout the city, and he would later be celebrated in that school's Hall of Fame. It so happened there was another Anthony Simone in one of his classes, therefore, teachers soon found it easier to call Dominic's son by the same name his classmates tossed around in the schoolyard. Once he became the big man on campus as a standout athlete, the nickname's tough and possibly mysterious edge seemed to fit his athletic prominence.

A scholarship beckoned at Appalachian State following high school, but Tex was uncertain as to whether he wanted to follow this path. Ahead, he knew, was mandatory armed forces service, which spared no able-bodied conscript, as its most famous recruit, Elvis Presley, would discover at the peak of his fame in the late 1950s. Tex ironically would have a near encounter with the King of Rock 'n Roll later in life, but, for the present, his only thought was of how to get through this necessary stage in his life.

Good Friend

Tex and Guy Desmascole grew up on the north side of Syracuse near Schiller Park. Desmascole recalled, "Tex and I would argue baseball all night. He was a Red Sox fan, and I was for the Yankees. But after all the arguing, there were no grudges, and we were still friends.

"We both went to North High School. It had once been a prison, then was a high school, and later became a seniors living center. Some people would say high school can be like a prison. But we played together on the football team. It was a really good team. We went undefeated one year. I remember a game against CBA (Christian Brothers Academy). I got a bloody nose and came out of the game, and the coach yelled at me, 'Where do you think you're going.' I said I'm injured, coach, and he just said, 'Get back in there, I like to see a red beak on a player every so often.' Later, Tex and me played football together on the Black and White team. We'd get together every Friday night during the season and talk football. I was always more of a football guy, Tex was the basketball player. I didn't play that game.

"I was drafted 4F near the end of the Second World War, but then it ended. The recruiting officer said, 'We'll get you eventually.' He was right! When the Korean War came along, I was one of the first to go. Tex wanted to go into the Navy, so he took the eye test and passed. My eyesight wasn't so good, so Tex told me what I should expect. I memorized the answers, but then they changed the chart, and I failed. So they put me in the army, and Tex came along with me even though he could have been in the Navy. Eventually, we were both sent to Germany, but we were in different outfits, so I didn't see as much of him there.

"After getting out of the service, we stood up for each other at our weddings. My wife and his wife were friends before they each got married and my wife actually introduced her friend to Tex. To this day, Wendy and John still call me Uncle Guy. In fact, I baptized Wendy at Our Lady of Pompei church. If I had to describe Tex, *He was a helluva guy.* You couldn't help liking him. He was quiet, but you always knew he was around. His parents were quiet people as well. His dad was a chef. They had a big family and were all close. I get tears just thinking about him.

"He'd see me in the stands at a ballgame and call to me, 'Why did you pay? I'd have got you in.' But I didn't want to take advantage of our friendship, and besides, I didn't mind paying; it helped keep the ball team financially healthy."

ARMY YEARS

The army years were central to Tex's later business acumen. He had enlisted with his north side gang and spent his first 15 months in the United States waiting for deployment (for which his letters home have been appended). He spent time in Vicksburg, Mississippi, with the Corps of Engineers learning how to build bridges, then it was on to Fort Dix in Trenton, New Jersey, and Fort Lee outside of Richmond, where he was educated in "The Army Way." Here, he earned his stripes as a Sergeant First Class. His yearning to learn and advance through the system was already apparent.

Once deployed to Nuremberg, Germany (his letters from there are also appended), he knew his infantry duty in Korea was only weeks away. Then fate intervened as authorities got wind of his sporting prowess in Syracuse. Just days before the platoon he commanded was ready to ship out, he was ordered by the "Old Man" to be transferred to Special Services, where he would be in command of the Army's sports teams. The teams played all of their championships at the site of the stadium, where Hitler had made speeches to millions of Germans.

The field had been renamed Nuremberg Soldiers Field, and Tex was in charge of cutting out softball, baseball, and football fields in the spacious stadium. He was responsible for scheduling, and he sometimes played in the Third Army Baseball and Softball Championships, the USFET (United States Forces European Theater) Track & Field Championships, along with the Archery and Horseshoe tournaments. One of the players he teamed with was former Cincinnati

Reds infielder Benny Zientara, who had played for his hometown Chiefs the season before.

Tex also coordinated Bob Hope's visit that included the singer and actress Gale Robbins. She often appeared with Hope at many military bases and later was in television episodes of *Gunsmoke, Perry Mason, 77 Sunset Strip,* and *The Untouchables.* Tex was also responsible for the Hal McIntyre Orchestra appearance and the Broadway Musical *Flying High,* which entertained the troops.

When the football season ended and winter loomed, the Old Man asked Tex if he knew anything about boxing. And, of course, he answered yes. His only knowledge of the sport was when he would travel to New York City as a kid to watch Joe Louis in Yankee Stadium or an up-and-coming welterweight named Carmen Basilio from Canastota, New York. Fortunately for Tex, another North Sider, Ray Rinaldi, from Syracuse, was in Germany at the same time. Ray gave Tex a quick lesson on training boxers, while at the same representing the team. Years later, the two of them teamed up to build a boxing center across the street from their old North High School, where youth were helped through Ray's educational program.

While sports kept Tex in Germany and away from Korea, he was laying the foundation for becoming an astute businessman. While there, he met Johnny Centrella from the Scranton, Pennsylvania area. Their friendship lasted for over 50 years. They were experts in acquiring items that Army GIs wanted, particularly cigarettes. The two did very well and even re-enlisted for an additional year to continue their entrepreneurship. Tex would send his earnings home to his brother Archie, who was instructed to give his mother a portion to help pay the bills; the rest was deposited in the bank. When Tex returned home, his bulging bank account allowed him to purchase his first automobile.

Years later, while traveling down Route 81 to watch the Chiefs play in Scranton, Tex was pulled over for speeding by a Pennsylvania State Trooper. The officer asked him for his license and registration. At first, the officer seriously quizzed him about some problematic issues regarding his army days and "acquiring items that Army GIs wanted most." Tex wondered where this might be going until the officer took off his shades, laughed, and revealed himself to be Tex's old buddy, Johnny Centrella. Years afterward, Tex sent Johnny an International League pass, allowing him to go to Scranton Red Barons games for free.

While he learned many life lessons in the Army, he attributed much of his business sense to those years in Germany. His only regret was that the platoon mates he trained hadn't been as fortunate as him. They had gone to Korea, and many of them didn't come back.

EVERYTHING CHANGES

After his army years in the United States and West Germany, Tex earned a business degree at Powelson Business Institute. "I always did like figures," he said. He became Bond Bread's office manager. In 1955, he married Joanna Venditti, a Syracuse girl he met at a wedding. He called her Joanne. They would have two children, Wendy and John. He continued taking night school accounting classes, certain his future was likely in the bread industry or a related field. He umpired local baseball games and was a pretty good bowler, but they all lacked the sporting challenges of his youth.

Then, minor league baseball returned to Syracuse.

Tex Simone's life, and that of his young family, was changed forever in 1961 by events north of the border. Not for the first time would a Canadian city play such an outsized role in Syracuse's baseball destiny. The Montreal Royals International League franchise dates back to 1928. French and English-speaking residents had been enthralled with baseball since the 19th century. The Royals had been saved from transfer or bankruptcy in the mid-1930s by the investment of a Quebecois entrepreneur who had made a small fortune selling his collection of gasoline stations to Imperial Oil. The team's angel, Charles Joseph Emile Trudeau, was a devoted baseball fan. In the early spring of 1935, he accompanied the Royals to their spring training site in Orlando. Cheering them on, he contracted a cold, leading to pneumonia, flu, and his sudden death. A stunned Montreal newspaper, *La Presse,* aptly dubbed him Quebec's "Apostle of Baseball."

However, his apostle-like financial, and one could say personal, sacrifice had allowed the Royals to survive, and by 1940, the Brooklyn Dodgers had become business partners and partial owners alongside Montreal's Quebecois management team. This opened a door for Branch Rickey's great experiment in breaking organized baseball's shameful color barrier. Here, in 1946, Jackie Robinson appeared in the uniform of the Montreal Royals, Brooklyn's chief farm team, and led them to the Little World Series title. The next year, Robinson joined the big league in Brooklyn and commenced his Hall of Fame major league career.

Nor was this Charles Joseph Emile Trudeau's only legacy, as his son Pierre, left fatherless at the age of 15, would later become Canada's 15th Prime Minister. At the all-star game in Montreal in 1982 Pierre Trudeau quipped that his late father would have been more impressed by him having a big league baseball career than leading the country. Years later, Tex would have a surprising encounter with Charles's grandson and another future Prime Minister.

Tex recalled having been in Toronto for a meeting with Syracuse's major league affiliate, the Blue Jays. "I was watching a game behind home plate at the team's old Exhibition Stadium, waiting to be called up for my meeting. I saw this young fellow in front of me who was apparently sitting by himself. We started talking and I noticed there appeared to be several eyes watching us closely. I finally asked him why he was there, and he said his dad was meeting with the team's owners. Of course, I then asked who his dad was, and he said the Prime Minister of Canada. That young fellow was Justin, who would become Canada's 23rd Prime Minister."

Montreal's demise was pre-ordained following the 1957 season with the transfer of their National League affiliate, the Brooklyn Dodgers, to Los Angeles. LA, in turn, wanted a Triple-A location closer to their West Coast home and so, despite an ownership position in Montreal, eventually abandoned the franchise to its fate. It had been a spectacular golden age until then. The flow of talent and multiple minor league titles seemed never-ending. It had coursed from Jackie Robinson and Duke Snider to Roy Campanella and Don Newcombe, and even its lesser stalwarts played historic roles with the Dodgers. They included Sandy Amoros, hero of Brooklyn's 1955 World Series victory, as well as Tommy Lasorda, the Royals ace with all-time franchise records in wins (107), games pitched (251), and innings pitched (1,461). He was a major league bust as a player but Los Angeles's future Hall of Fame manager.

Unfortunately, minor league baseball was in the doldrums through the 1950s. Having over-expanded after the war, it was now seriously retrenching, with towns, cities, and even leagues disappearing from once-promising markets. As well, there was the increasing novelty of televised major league games. For its part, the International League was realizing its future lay increasingly in mid-size cities unlikely ever to attract Major League Baseball. No place better fits this prescription than Syracuse, New York. Much smaller in comparison to Montreal, Syracuse's major league pretensions were in decline. Their National Basketball Association (NBA) Nationals franchise, renowned for players Dolph Schayes and Paul Seymour, and owner Danny Biasone, with all of whom Tex had ties, had only a few remaining years in the city before moving to Philadelphia. Syracuse's lone Major League Baseball entity was a 19th-century memory.

Despite Montreal's leading attendance in the post-war boom years, crowds had declined more recently, and the team's local owners were unwilling to shoulder more losses.

Attempts to find a Quebec-based investor for the Montreal Royals International League franchise were led by the League's one-time President, Frank Shaughnessy, who had made the Canadian city region of two million his home.

Syracuse's re-entry into the International League in 1961 would be at the somewhat sordid expense of those Royals after Frank Shaughnessy's request for more time to find local investors was summarily rejected. Ostensibly, it was because, with only two and half months remaining before the 1961 season opener, the League was unwilling to risk assuming even temporary ownership. Syracuse was dangling a rent-free offer for the use of MacArthur Stadium as op-posed to the $50,000 rental fee in Montreal. Moving the franchise to Syracuse would save league members $30,000 in travel expenses. Finally, Buffalo greedily stood to inherit Montreal's schedule, which included 11 Sunday dates and two holidays, but like Toronto, they would start on the road for the first two weeks of the season before opening at home on May 3rd. The International League was so anxious to abandon their long-time partner that its president, Tommy Richardson, said they might have to operate the transplanted team if the $100,000 drive for community ownership in Syracuse was not successful, cynically the very fate they wanted to avoid in Montreal. The move to Syracuse was quickly approved.

There was the little matter of what to do with an entire ensemble of baseball-related items from Montreal with the Royals' name on them. The uniforms had once been worn by future Dodgers. It's even possible one of those might have been used by Jackie Robinson. Syracuse had opted not to continue with the Royals name, favoring instead the local sobriquet, the Chiefs. Political correctness was not as yet a factor in name choice as it would become. In any case, the Syracuse Chiefs had no need in 1961 for uniforms bearing the Royals' name. They were stored for years until one day, as Tex recalled, "The nickname of the local Catholic high school Assumption, near where I grew up, was the Royals, so I passed on those aptly named baseball shirts, pants, and stockings to them where no doubt they were used until they wore out and were then tossed. Who knows how much such memorabilia would have been worth in later years?"

Baseball Returns to Syracuse

Minnesota Twins, themselves having just relocated from Washington where they were the American League's perennial losing Senators, signed an agreement with the Syracuse team in which they agreed to pay the manager's salary, spring training costs, and the transportation of players to and from the south. They also initially stocked the Syracuse roster with 18 players, while Los Angeles sent eight more to fill out the lineup. Don Labbruzzo came over from Buffalo and became the club's chief executive.

Meanwhile, a plant manager at a bread company, who had recently been confirmed as an eligible candidate for the county job of bookkeeper with an annual salary of $5,575 or a city job with a $4,900 maximum, was having second thoughts about his career choices. He really wanted to get involved with the new baseball franchise. If he learned anything from watching this murky transfer business at both the major and minor league levels, it was how little sentimentality there was among owners and league executives. Heck, even one of the most storied names in baseball and, next to the Yankees, its most successful team over a ten-year period, the Brooklyn Dodgers, had been uprooted for even greater riches in Los Angeles. The New York borough of Brooklyn never received a replacement team.

One day, possibly in the not-too-distant future, Syracuse might be victim of this same unhappy franchise fate suffered by Brooklyn and, at the minor league level, Montreal. Just maybe he could make a difference. He believed his athletic background, military experience, and the business acumen attained in the Service could benefit a sporting entity in which he truly believed. If he did not act now, an opportunity might never come again.

Lifetime chum Guy Desmascole described Tex's road to the Chiefs. "You might say my wife got Tex started with the baseball team. Her brother was a groundskeeper for the team after they moved here from Montreal in 1961. Myself and Tex would help him out. In fact, we'd go in the morning to prepare the field so my brother-in-law wouldn't have to come in that early. Tex got to know everyone, including the president of the team, so when an opportunity came up to be more involved, Tex was in the right place at the right time. And he sure took advantage of it. Guys would leave, and he'd fill in and eventually get that job."

"I was 32," Tex says, "I wasn't happy. Disgruntled, you could say. I needed to make a career change. I quit Bond Bread and started out on the grounds crew at MacArthur Stadium. Joanne couldn't understand how I could go from a white-collar job to the grounds crew of a professional baseball team. There's only one word to describe my reasoning. I call it love, as in L-O-V-E. It wasn't easy. I worked in the clubhouse at night after the games, assisting the trainer and making a little from clubhouse dues to help support my family."

At home, he told Joanne he might not even be able to put bread on the table, a perk, along with a salary, afforded by his plant manager job. Despite the reality of their raising two infants, she agreed to his move. In so doing, she and Tex changed the fortunes of baseball in Syracuse while guaranteeing its long-term sustainability. It provided many years of front-line engagement by his family. This was a reward as meaningful as the eventual financial one of a full-time job.

Joanne recalls, "I was a little upset, but the office manager job wasn't for him. Baseball was what he wanted, and I went along with it. Those were lean years, but we managed. Our mothers chipped in. I babysat my girl friend's little boy for maybe $10 a week. We watched our pennies. You can do anything if you really want to."

In giving up a well-paying, secure, prestigious, but mundane and not particularly glamorous job for what was effectively a volunteer, non-paying role at the lowest rung of the Syracuse Chiefs' organization, Tex knew he might not even be part of their staffing structure. There was no guarantee of long-term employment. Fate would soon intervene.

STEPS ON THE LADDER
OF SUCCESS

I t was not long before Tex's unpaid grounds-crew role was supplemented, thanks to his experience as a muscle massager in the armed forces. Chiefs General Manager Don Labbruzzo provided Tex with a small stipend for him to assist trainer Rudy Alfonso. Then, fate intervened.

Alfonso suffered a heart attack in June, and Tex was his emergency full-time replacement for a twelve-day road trip while also assuming the job of road secretary. It was not the easiest work. At the beginning of the month, players and the coaching staff had almost come to blows when the team was told they'd be taking the 240-mile trip to Toronto by bus to play that city's International League team, the Maple Leafs.

The turmoil had led to the departure of the Chiefs' field leadership. Infielder Frank Verdi stepped in as interim manager. His coaches were catcher Dutch Dotterer, a one-time Schiller Park playmate of Tex's, and first baseman Joe Altobelli, a future World Series-winning manager with Baltimore in 1983. These friendships continued throughout Tex's life. Within a year, Tex's gamble of forsaking the bread industry for baseball was rewarded because of another man's bad fortune. At season end, Alfonso's doctor advised the former trainer not to resume the job owing to the stress.

In early January 1962, Tex's brief assumption of the trainer and road secretary jobs was made permanent. He took advantage of learning as much as possible from his nearby access to Julie Reichel, the veteran athletic trainer at Syracuse University, renowned for its football, basketball, and lacrosse teams. In January, the Chiefs sent Tex to Gus Mauch's highly acclaimed Florida-based School of Athletic Training in Kissimmee, run in conjunction with a baseball clinic. Mauch had been a trainer with the Yankees and the football Giants before joining the expansion New York Mets.

Tex borrowed money from family members to make the trip to Florida. His daughter Wendy recalls, "We were very poor at the time. Dad was not making much in his new career, so he looked in the paper to see if anyone needed their car driven down to Florida. He found an elderly lady who needed just that! He delivered the car to St. Petersburg and took a bus over to the training school. He had three meals a day and a bed in a barracks, but he was used to this from his Army days. He attended classes in the morning and college games in the afternoon.

"Gus Mauch took a liking to him and invited Dad to the Mets' spring training camp in February at Miller Huggins Field. He wanted Dad to work as his assistant. So, my dad found another car heading north and drove it back to Syracuse. When he arrived home, he told Mom she had to pack us up, and we had three days to get back to Florida for a Major League Spring Training camp. Luckily, my mom knew how much this meant to Dad, so she agreed. We arrived back in Florida just five days after Dad first left. This time, however, we stayed at the Major League hotel."

It would have been easy for this young man to have been starstruck. What an experience it was to check in with renowned baseball personalities like Casey Stengel, Rogers Hornsby, Red Cress, Cookie Lavaggetto, Gil Hodges, Richie Ashburn, and Red Ruffing. As it turned out, Tex's most important duty might have been sitting next to Casey Stengel in the dugout. "Casey was a darling of the newspaper guys, but sometimes he'd doze off during a game," Tex later recalled, "Now, in his seventies, Casey was worried the photographers might catch him taking one of those naps. My job was to nudge him ever so slightly if I saw the media coming."

Tex's Syracuse Chiefs boss, Don Labbruzzo, said, "Tex did such a good job down there, Mauch wanted him to be his assistant with the Mets. Tex refused because of his allegiance to the Chiefs. But we wouldn't have stood in his way. He really is big league in his profession." It was the first of many times a major league team offered Tex a job. "He's a rare fellow," Labbruzzo continued, "He's about as fine a person as anyone I've known – morally strong, honest, energetic, and intelligent."

So accomplished was Simone that when the Chiefs became Detroit's farm team in 1963, Labbruzzo convinced Tigers' General Manager Jim Campbell not to replace Tex with one of their own trainers. A few years later, the Tigers offered the Syracuse trainer the opportunity to join their major league setup. For a second time, Tex would decide to remain at home. Back in Syracuse, field manager Frank Carswell added his favorable comments, "He's a real help to me. Our feelings coincide. It's a good relationship. I appreciate the man very much. Tex is a guy who thinks that a player ought to stay in the ball game even if he doesn't feel like it. He did a great service to Mack Jones in encouraging and kidding him out of what Mack thought were serious injuries or ailments."

It was a different time and place in America, an era of the **Green Book** when African Americans relied on this famous guide for information on gas stations, stores, and hotels that would service them. "I learned a lot about racism in those years with New York and Detroit," Tex recalled. "On every road trip, my job was getting the players checked into their hotel. Some cities did not permit our black and white players to stay in the same one. I'd have to tell the black players to stay on the bus while I checked the white players into their hotel. I then took the black players to theirs.

"When we were working with the Mets, Outfielder Joe Christopher pleaded with me to take him back to the white hotel. I asked him why, and he said he wasn't black because he'd been born in the Virgin Islands. Fortunately, one of the great stars of the International League, Luke Easter, a one-time player with the famous Homestead

Grays in the last days of the Negro Leagues, was in the lobby. I asked for his help. Easter took Christopher aside and told him in blunt terms, 'It doesn't matter what country you are from; your skin is the same as mine.' Joe learned a very sad lesson."

One of Tex's finest memories of this time was an invitation from the Tigers after the 1964 season to watch over their young players in Puerto Rico playing winter ball for the Mayagüez Indians. He was able to bring along his young family. The team was owned by a wealthy businessman, Babel Pérez. Bob Swift managed the team. His players, many part of the future 1968 World Series champions, included Denny McLain, Jim Northrup, Mickey Stanley, Willie Horton, along with Joe Christopher, Ozzie Virgil Sr., and Julio Cotay, among others.

Tex said, "Some of the players were making more there than they did in the United States. We were housed in an apartment complex owned by Pérez minutes from the downtown and the beach. Apparently, I was the first non-local trainer to work in the Puerto Rican Winter League. It was an honor, and the money was great. Many of the visiting American players on other teams wandered over to our clubhouse for treatment. I was their confidante, confessor, and the guy between the manager and the players. Every day, I took my daughter Wendy (age 6) to school in the morning and then my son John (age 3) to the town square for freshly cut oranges. I even went with some of the ballplayers to gamble at the local cockfights."

It was not all peace and happiness, however. Having beaten Arecibo in the semi-finals, the losing hometown fans attacked the visitors' bus with rocks and sugar cane. A boulder shattered the glass and hit Tex, who wound up in hospital having glass removed from his eye. Jim Northrup suggested they all get down on the floor like Ozzie Virgil had warned, "They'll probably start shooting their guns next." Another popular story had Denny McLain suggesting to owner Pérez that his pitching could either win or lose the championship game and questioned what additional incentive the owner would provide. McLain won the game and got his extra pay.

In 1965, Tex got a taste of the majors when the Tigers' long-time trainer, Jack Homel, returned home to California in July following severe wildfires after his own home was lost. Tex remained with the Tigers until season's end. The experience of living in an increasingly troubled city soon to be torn by riots and fires may have been an additional reason he preferred the relative peace of Syracuse. After the 1966 season, the Tigers and Yankees flipped their affiliations. Detroit moved over to Toledo, Ohio, and the Yankees settled in Syracuse. One final attempt to get him to come to Detroit in an office job was rejected, but this may have been due to the opportunity of working, even at somewhat of a distance, with the New York Yankees.

Those Yankees were in a steep decline from the years of glory between 1949 and 1964 when they reached the World Series in all but two years. Mickey Mantle and Whitey Ford were nearing the end of their respective careers. There were few upcoming gems to share with Syracuse, and the Triple-A team suffered as a result. Perhaps most notably, Jim Bouton's major league pitching career was no longer up to its one-time 20-win capability. He pitched 16 games for the Chiefs, posting a 2-8 record, while dabbling in a future career for which he became noted, authoring *Ball Four*.

IT'S THE PEOPLE
YOU MEET

Tex's business-like nature was underlined by an essential gentleness of disposition, allowing him never to think he was better than anyone else. Working his way up in the trainer's role, he recalled when Ray Oyler was laid up by a perforated ulcer late in the 1964 season. "I was close to Ray, and it was like my brother was in trouble. I even held his hand while they were rolling him into the operating room." Best remembered as a slick-fielding but weak-hitting shortstop, Oyler later backed up Mickey Stanley in Detroit's 1968 World Series championship run. Medical issues continued to haunt him, and he was only 42 when he died.

In 1967, after the Chiefs left the Detroit Tigers organization and began their association with the New York Yankees, Tex was invited by Joe Soares, the Yankees athletic trainer, to attend their major league camp and get to know the players. It was Tex's sixth big-league camp, so by then, he knew the drill. On arrival, Soares told Tex to put his clothes in the locker over in the corner. Tex did as he was told, but he noticed there was a full uniform already there. Soares said, "Don't worry, just push them to the other side."

Part of the team's tradition was the attendance at spring training in a special instructor role of many of the Yankee greats from the past. This year, it was Joe DiMaggio. He'd been retired for over 15 years but came back in 1967 as a favor to his good friend Ralph Houk. Ralph was never going to win a personality contest. He gathered the team and staff to remind all of them that Mr. DiMaggio was coming and that no one was allowed to ask for his autograph. "He is here to work and help you guys get better," Houk proclaimed. Still, Tex was excited to meet the Yankee great. He had grown up a Red Sox fan, but for a kid from Syracuse's North side and one whose father was born in Italy – Joe DiMaggio was a god.

When DiMaggio walked into the clubhouse in Ft. Lauderdale, he talked briefly with Joe Soares, who told him where his locker was. Tex was working hard nearby, trying not to be too eager to introduce himself. Minutes later, he heard someone loudly yelling that somebody's equipment was in his locker. Soares told Tex to find out what the commotion was about. Tex saw that not only was it Joe DiMaggio who was yelling, but he was standing in front of the locker where Tex's clothes were hanging. He knew immediately whose uniform Joe Soares had told him to push over to the side. It was a setup for the new guy!

Tex apologized profusely to DiMaggio and told him he would remove his stuff immediately. DiMaggio stopped him and said, "Tex, they got you good, didn't they? Don't you dare move your stuff; I'm only here for two weeks. We will locker together." Never did Tex imagine he would be this close to the Yankee Clipper and would share a locker with him as well. They became good friends during those two weeks. DiMaggio, without asking, signed a number of baseballs and gave them to Tex for his Yankee friends back home. On DiMaggio's last day, and as manager Ralph Houk was walking by the two, the Yankee Clipper said loud enough for all to hear, "Hey Tex, I put the autographed balls in a sock in your locker. Let me know if you need any more." Houk, probably in on the joke, glared at Tex and just kept walking.

In 1978, Tex and his son John met DiMaggio at the Baseball Winter Meetings in Orlando. John was attending Valencia College, and he and his dad ran into the Yankee Great in one of the hotel bars. John recalled, "Joe remembered my father from the 1967 spring camp and, looking at me, said, 'So I guess you would like my autograph.'

Nervously, I responded, 'No, thank you, Mr. DiMaggio. I have a few balls and photos signed by you to me already.' Not many people turn down the offer of an autograph from Joe DiMaggio."

A few years later, John got the opportunity to repay his father for this meeting with a baseball legend. The Chiefs had entered into a working agreement with the Toronto Blue Jays for the 1978 season. Pat Gillick had hired Bobby Doerr as a hitting coach. As a child, Tex had cheered for the Red Sox, and his favorite player was Doerr. Immediately, he made sure Pat introduced Bobby to him at the club's spring training home in Dunedin. The two became great friends over the years.

In 1983, John Simone was asked to help Pat Gillick run the Blue Jays' spring training camp after the minor league administrator, Elliott Wahle, had left the team to lead the Toys "R" Us Company in Canada. One of John's responsibilities was to coordinate the spring training games at home and on the road for the team's four minor league affiliates. Tex usually spent a week or so in Dunedin to check on the team and see if the coaching staff needed anything before the trip back to Syracuse. While he was there, the Chiefs were scheduled to play the Red Sox Triple-A team in Winter Haven.

Bobby Doerr was planning to make the trip to see his friend Ted Williams, who was coaching the Red Sox minor league players. John says, "I immediately thought that this could be the greatest day of my dad's professional baseball career if I could set up a meeting through Bobby. Before he boarded the bus, I told Bobby that next to him, Ted Williams was Tex's favorite. Could you introduce my dad to Ted? Without hesitation, Doerr said yes.

"I told my dad he had to go to Winter Haven that day, so we drove over, arriving just before noon. Bobby met him and asked Tex to come with him as he wanted to introduce Tex to a close friend of his. As we walked to the backfields of the Red Sox minor league complex, we saw a coach sitting in the bleachers watching a few Red Sox minor leaguers take extra batting practice. Bobby yelled out his name, and my father was speechless. After the two old Red Sox hugged and shook hands, Bobby Doerr said, 'Ted, this is my very good friend Tex Simone; he runs the Syracuse club.' As that day went on and the minor league games were being played on other fields, I would glance over to the bleachers and see Ted Williams, Bobby Doerr, and Tex Simone together laughing and talking. I knew it was something he would never forget. I know I never did."

MORE CHANGES TO TEX'S
IMPROVING STATUS

By 1968, losses both on the field and in the team's bank account were threatening the team's survival in Syracuse. A much bigger city, and one which eventually became their major league affiliate, had lost its International League team at the end of the 1967 season. Toronto's League connection stretched back into the 19th century. There were few guarantees and almost no sentimentality associated with the manner in which a local team could move or simply go out of business.

Syracuse GM Don Labbruzzo was by now deeply impressed at the work ethic of his 39-year-old trainer and traveling secretary. Perhaps he could see the need for fresh blood and energy to stir any cobwebs the Chiefs might have taken on despite the relatively brief time since their return to Triple-A baseball. Tex was appointed the team's Business Manager. For Tex, it meant a move from a field job as a trainer to the front office. Already committed to another spring training in Fort Lauderdale with the Yankees, Tex put the decision on hold until the start of the season. At the big league camp, Whitey Ford retired and became the pitching coach, and Mickey Mantle was playing in his final season.

"It was a hard decision," Tex recalled, "But after returning from spring training, I began handling the team's business manager responsibilities as well as assisting our new trainer, Jerry McCann. Once the season opened, Labbruzzo added more responsibilities to my job description. As well as handling the team's business, I was now in charge of public relations." Effectively, Tex had become Labbruzzo's Assistant General Manager.

At season end, Tex was invited to Detroit to watch the Tigers play the St. Louis Cardinals in the World Series. Many of the Tigers players that had come through Syracuse and Detroit management under Jim Campbell had not forgotten the role their one-time trainer had played. Mickey Lolich won all three starts, outdueling Hall of Famer Bob Gibson, and the Tigers won in seven games.

"1969 was the first year I was not in Florida in March," Tex said. "My front office duties were expanding, and we had a new trainer, Gene Monahan, who had just graduated from Indiana University. He had begun his career with the Yankees, oddly enough, as a batboy in 1962. While in school, he worked at a number of jobs in player development. Geno worked for three years in Syracuse from 1969-71 before eventually moving up to the Yankees as their Head Athletic Trainer [he retired in 2011]."

Financial challenges continued into 1969. Frank Verdi was back as field manager. His major league playing career lasted one game in 1953 when he replaced Phil Rizzuto at shortstop. He made it to the on-deck circle later in that game before a third out prevented him from getting a major league at-bat. In 1959, as a player with the International League Rochester Red Wings, Verdi was struck in the head by a stray bullet during a game against the Havana Sugar Kings. Cubans were celebrating the recent revolution by firing off guns outside the ballpark. Verdi had assumed the third base coaching duties when manager Cot Veal was ejected from the game. Still wearing the plastic lining in his hat from playing that night, a bullet deflected off his head and lodged in his shoulder, causing a minor injury.

If that was not a serious enough omen for the new Syracuse executive, the night of May 14th had an even bigger one. A few hours after the Chiefs lost 7-3 to the Red Wings, Tex got a call as he was preparing for bed. His place of business for the past nine years was up in flames. "By the time I got there, a large part of our once majestic stadium had been reduced to rubble. Gone were the team's offices, concession stands, and the press box. The entire center of the stadium had been destroyed. I supposed we could have tossed in the towel had we been so inclined, but it also brought out the best in our minor league partners. We spent the next month on the road. Sam Nader, the owner of the Oneonta team and himself a Yankees Rookie League affiliate, made sure we were able to play some home games without disrupting our International League season. Repairs to the stadium took longer than expected, however, and we moved the remainder of the games in June to Auburn, just 40 minutes from Central New York. By opening his stadium to our use, Leo Pinckney, the President of the Auburn Baseball team, gave us a much-needed opportunity to generate some income to pay the bills. "When we returned to Syracuse in early July, only about 4,000 seats remained, and the offices were replaced by a trailer with temporary concession stands scattered about," Tex recalled.

A well-known idiom goes something like the following, "If I didn't have bad luck, I'd have no luck at all." Tex had every reason to feel this way, but his philosophy was a testament to always looking on the bright side of life. Somewhere in his memory, he might have recalled a North High School physics lesson on Isaac Newton's third law of motion. "For every action, there is an equal and opposite reaction." In the organization's moment of greatest despair, suddenly, their team took off in the standings.

"Under Verdi," Tex said, "We finished with a 75-65 record, just three games out of first. Frank was always looking for an edge and recommended a number of moves during the season. These changed our fortunes. Lefthanded hitting Dave MacDonald hit 24 home runs and drove in a team-leading 82 runs. By the next year, he was sharing a 1970 Topps Rookie Stars baseball card with a future Yankee great. Then, we picked up lefthanded pitcher Rob Gardner, who was 0-6 with a 6.04 ERA at Portland in the Pacific Coast League. He went 6-4 with three saves down the stretch. Rob returned to play in Syracuse on several occasions afterward."

With the Vietnam War still raging, the Chiefs had a number of players requiring service in the Reserves. Over the years, the rules had changed, and in 1969, one of their players was serving four days a week at Fort Drum, 80 miles north of Syracuse. He was able to play on the weekends. "He was the rookie star on that baseball card with Dave McDonald ... Thurman Munson from Akron, Ohio," Tex recalled. "He'd been drafted by the Yankees the year before and played 71 games in the 1968 season at Double-A Binghampton. Munson got in 28 games for us in 1969. I'd drive up to Watertown once a week, pick him up for a series of games, and then return him to his base. An old childhood friend of mine, Sam Grillo, was serving as the base's acting Colonel in charge of all personnel release. The Colonel was also a big baseball fan and had helped the club and the Yankees in the past with players including Roy White, Bobby Murcer, and Stan Bahnsen.

"The Munson situation was different; the Yankees were actually good in 1969. They were challenging the Baltimore Orioles for the American League Pennant. Manager Ralph Houk wanted Munson for as much time as he could get him. On several occasions, my trips back from Watertown were diverted to the Syracuse airport for a quick flight to Yankee Stadium for weekend games. Colonel Grillo made sure the Commander's television was otherwise occupied for those 26 games."

For their part, the Chiefs made the playoffs for the first time since 1964, and their opponent was the Louisville Colonels, the top AAA team of the Boston Red Sox. The series went five games with the deciding game played at burnt-out MacArthur Stadium. With the game tied 3-3 in the top of the 10th inning, Louisville catcher Bob Montgomery came up with the bases loaded and crushed a ball to deep center field, where Chiefs centerfielder Jim Lyttle made one of the greatest catches in stadium history. His over-the-shoulder grab kept the game tied at three runs apiece.

In the bottom of the 10th, light-hitting Chiefs shortstop Frank Baker was the unlikely hero. He came into the game as a .244 hitter and had only two home runs all season. He sent the first pitch from the Louisville pitcher over the old scoreboard in right field for the dramatic victory. The Chiefs then took on the Columbus Jets in the Championship round and defeated them four games to one, capturing their first Governor's Cup since 1954.

More Changes

General Manager Don Labbruzzo left Syracuse at season end to help revitalize the Buffalo franchise, themselves desperately in need of help. He could not save them, and they would move to Winnipeg in 1970 as the Montreal Expos Triple-A farm team. In Syracuse, on the other hand, the organization was on a high coming off a championship season, but besides their GM's departure and the gaping hole in the center of the stadium's seating, the team was staring at a financial hole of over $200,000. The team's Board of Directors, led by a local banker and Chairman of the Board, Anthony Henninger, and the club's new President, Donald Waful, an insurance agent, turned to Tex Simone to find a business solution for the team's precarious status. Still uncertain if Tex should have overall authority, they also appointed fellow board member Kenneth Leach as effectively a Co-General Manager. Tex represented the team at all league meetings while handling the team's day-to-day business. Leach reported on Tex's progress at monthly Board meetings. The team had approached Dutch Dotterer's father (also Dutch) about the combined GM job, but he was unequivocal. "Hire Tex," he said, "He's the best man for the job!"

Within a year and a half after leaving his on-field trainer's role, Tex was the team's top man in everything but title. Fate once again intervened in Tex's favor. The 1970 season was filled with many challenges. Improving the team's finances was priority number one, while repairing a stadium destroyed by fire was a close second. Tex worked closely with Henninger, the Board Chair and a one-time Syracuse mayor. Despite limited cash reserves, Henninger arranged for the four largest banks in the area to provide the team with a $50,000 loan.

The baseball season was quickly approaching. Optimism was high. Frank Verdi was returning for his third season. The team's relationship as the Yankees affiliate could not have been better. Tex hit it off immediately with Yankees General Manager Lee McPhail and the Player Development staff under Clyde Kluttz. McPhail was the son of Cincinnati Reds and Brooklyn Dodgers executive Larry McPhail, whose own post-World War I exploits had included a failed attempt to capture Kaiser Wilhelm at his Netherlands hideout and present him to the Allied forces for trial. His son Lee began his career with the Yankees in 1945 and then left to work for the Baltimore Orioles in 1958. He returned to the Yankees in 1966, two years removed from their last World Series appearance. McPhail would end his Yankees career in 1973 after George Steinbrenner purchased the team from CBS.

The 1970 Yankees were contenders again with the emergence of eventual Rookie of the Year Thurman Munson and All-Star outfielders Bobby Murcer and Roy White. Fritz Peterson would win 20 games, and Lindy McDaniel would save 29 as the Bronx Bombers finished with 93 wins and a second-place finish, their best since 1964. The team in Syracuse was equally talented with a number of players returning, some for their third season. New to the team were veterans Bobby Cox and Bill Robinson. Cox was nearing the end of his playing career, having just spent the past two seasons as the Yankees' third baseman, replacing Clete Boyer in that position in 1968. Robinson, 27, had spent the past three years with the Yankees. Both hoped to revive their careers. The Chiefs won the city's first International League Pennant behind Verdi's masterful use of veteran players and youngsters like Yankees prospect Ron Blomberg. Syracuse baseball was due for a huge payday as they breezed through the International League playoffs, defeating the Tidewater Tides and then the Columbus Jets, capturing their second consecutive Governor's Cup Championship. Normally, this would have been the season's end, but in 1970, Triple-A baseball once again instituted a Junior World Series with the champions of the International League and American Association meeting.

The Chiefs' opponent was the Omaha Royals managed by Jack McKeon. The teams were to play the first two games at Omaha's historic Rosenblatt Stadium and then return to Syracuse to play games three, four, and five if necessary. Tropical Storm Felice was hovering over Nebraska, so the two teams sat for three days before International League President George Sisler, Jr. moved the entire series to Syracuse. The Syracuse franchise was promised a financial windfall.

"We won the first two before Omaha took game three. Before game four, however, I had my first major challenge in this new executive role," Tex recalled. "While the players, now playing for two weeks in September, were receiving an extra paycheck from their respective teams, they wanted a share of the gate receipts. Both teams were prepared to boycott game four and the series. The threat was real. Game time was at 7:30 pm, and the players had not left the clubhouse. They were still discussing their options. Understanding the situation that they had put me in as their rookie general manager, veteran players Len Boehmer and Bobby Cox intervened and averted a crisis. The players received additional revenue, paid out from the league's share. The agreement did not cost our Syracuse club any money, but it opened my eyes to the business side of baseball now that I had moved from the clubhouse to the front office."

Tex understood the players' request, but he was disturbed that his manager, Frank Verdi, did not step in, instead telling the players to work it out. The team would win game four and then celebrate on the field at old MacArthur Stadium as they defeated the Omaha Royals for the Little World Series title. Verdi was named the International League and Minor League Baseball Manager of the Year. Rob Gardner picked up four playoff wins for a twenty-win season. Tex Simone was named the International League's Executive of the Year.

Most importantly, the team made a large profit. All debt was eliminated from the previous nine years of the operation. The Chiefs were on their way. The Tex Simone era officially began in

1961, but 1970 marked a real marker in the sand for a career of accomplishment, reaching another 43 years into the future. Before year-end, Tex Simone had become the team's one and only General Manager, overseen now only by a community Board of Directors. 1970 would be the high point of on-field accomplishment in Tex's long career, but in the Minor Leagues, other priorities play just as big or a bigger role.

Optimism for the 1971 season was high. As the calendar turned to February, Yankees General Manager Lee McPhail contacted Tex concerning Frank Verdi's managerial situation in Syracuse. Verdi was not budging on his worth for another season in Syracuse. With either side unwilling to move, McPhail allowed Tex to handle negotiations. In the end, it came down to $500 a month. Tex told Verdi the Chiefs would pick up the difference. Verdi told Tex it was not Syracuse's responsibility to pay him. "Tell Lee to get himself another manager." Lee McPhail did just that.

McPhail eventually turned to Loren Babe, who played for the Yankees in the 50s and then managed in the minor leagues from 1961-66, spending the 1966 season with Toledo in the International League. Loren Babe was named the Chiefs' manager that spring, and Frank Verdi returned home to Long Island to spend his first season out of baseball since 1945.

Business Stability

From the time of his installation as General Manager in 1970, Tex spent over forty years creating business stability for Syracuse's minor league Chiefs. He had started in an era when such franchises had no guarantee of success or even survival. Even major league teams struggled to fill empty seats. By expanding the range of promotions and reasons for spectators to make a return visit to MacArthur Stadium, he at first upset many of those same major league organizations. Tex said, "They described us as carnival workers, making a farce of the game by our use of unconventional enticements. Ten years later, they were all doing the same."

During this time, he continued to deal with the impact of the catastrophic fire, which had wiped out the entire central seating portion of the stadium. "A promoter for Elvis Presley approached us about The King performing here but asked about what appeared to be a hole in the middle of the stadium. After I told him about the fire and the absence of seating there, we never heard from him again."

Eventually, Tex got MacArthur's central portion rebuilt and the rest of the ballpark upgraded so that, for a time, it was considered one of the better minor league facilities. Onondaga County provided $3 million in funding for the rebuild, but as Tex later noted, the franchise annually pumped that amount back into the local economy. The ball club handled operational expenses but depended on the county if major works were necessary. "If the Chiefs ever left town," Simone said, "It would be like a big factory closing."

OPENING DAY

Opening Day would always be Tex's favorite time on the baseball calendar. That's when a new and returning crop of players took the field, some up from Single and Double-A, others were aging veterans hoping to get another shot at the "show," and lastly were the returning prospects not seen since the past September, but all of them hoping for a mid-season call-up to the big team. For a minor league team, all of the hard work over the winter months of selling season tickets and outfield sign space, recruiting new sponsors, and ensuring the return of long-time supporters was on display. John Simone recalled the first task assigned to him by his father on his first day in the front office. "I showed up at 9 in the morning, and Tex gave me a stack of ad brochures and blank contracts. He told me to get out of the office, hit the streets, and don't come back until 4:30." John found out quite quickly that in the office, the boss was Tex, not Dad.

For Opening Day, the field at MacArthur Stadium had to be specially groomed, cleared of winter's detritus, places patched where the grass had not returned to its green bounty, and finally ensuring the base paths maintained their crucial mix of sand, clay, and silt. The mound had to be just the right height, the concession stands well-stocked for a hungry and thirsty big crowd, and even the washrooms had to perform after a winter of non-use. One year, they checked on the condition of the lone toilet in the umpires' room. "When we turned it on," Tex said at the time, "The bottom blew out. I'm still trying to find a new toilet to fit that hole. It's one of those that fits in the wall, not on the floor. I guess I have one more day to locate one."

All of this could go sideways if the weather, one of the few things over which Tex had no control, refused to cooperate. It might snow or be warm enough for shorts, but in April, rain is always the big concern. Catastrophe was impending one year just before opening day when the team's eight-year-old tarp, in Tex's words, "Leaked like a sieve." All of Tex's formidable experience in baseball, going back to his army days in Germany as a talented finder of generally un-available items, was challenged. "Then, I had a brainstorm," he said, "I called Cooperstown, which had just one game a year, the Hall of Fame game. They had their tarp stored away in a barn and very gra-ciously let us borrow it. We had to send a large flat-bed truck owned by a friend of mine named Tony Santaro to get it. Then, it took a der-rick at each end to load and unload it. But a tarp's very important to us. It can save you a ballgame."

Saving a ballgame was a lesson John learned close to his first day on the job. Tex knew that for a minor league franchise, the bottom line was as important as, or more so, than the baselines. His philoso-phy was simple but foolproof. "You set yourself up a budget and pre-pare for the worst, then at least you'll break even. Then, if you have a winning club, it's frosting on the cake. If you have a mediocre club, at least the cake can be eaten without choking."

THE TORONTO BLUE JAYS

I n 1978, Tex convinced his Board to drop the elite and local fan favorite New York Yankees for an affiliation with the expansion Toronto Blue Jays, who were only entering their second year of American League play. Years before, Tex had demonstrated the tough side of this personality when he stood up to George Steinbrenner, who told Tex he controlled all aspects of Syracuse's baseball operation. "Actually, Mr. Steinbrenner," he replied, "Because we're a New York Yankees Triple-A affiliate, you do control the player development function, but as a community-owned team, all other business decisions are ones we control and make."

By 1977, Tex could see the writing on the wall. It appeared to be only a matter of time before Steinbrenner ditched Syracuse for an affiliation with a team in his native State of Ohio. "We made a decision about what our future would be like without George Steinbrenner and the Yankees before they made a decision about not being with us. If he'd even visited once in the previous year or shown any interest, it might have made a difference," Tex recalled.

If there was a last straw, it was the circumstances surrounding the New York Yankees making their final appearance at MacArthur Stadium. As the Triple-A minor league affiliate of the Yankees an annual exhibition game by the Bronx Bombers in Syracuse was a major event. Such games, though they meant nothing in the standings, were an essential money-maker for any minor league franchise. Tickets went on sale from the moment the date was announced. Mickey Mantle had made appearances in this game back in 1967 and

1968. Crowds of over 14,000 packed MacArthur Stadium. For many, it was a once-in-a-lifetime opportunity to see a true legend.

In 1977, the Yankees were coming off a four game World Series loss to the Cincinnati Reds. To get over the final hump in their return to the glory days of the 1950s and early 60s, they signed Reggie Jackson and Don Gullett. Along with a lineup featuring Catfish Hunter, Thurman Munson, Sparky Lyle, Bucky Dent, Craig Nettles, and Chris Chambliss, a sellout of Mantle proportions was anticipated.

George Steinbrenner, the Yankees owner often simply referred to as "The Boss," viewed the obligation as an unnecessary distraction. He was prepared to cancel it. Gabe Paul, his General Manager, contacted Tex on Easter Sunday that season and broke the news about George's intentions. Tex was advised to get on a plane to New York the next day and make his case. For his part, Paul made an appointment for Tex to meet George and emphasize the importance of the game to his minor league franchise and city.

Tex flew into New York on the first plane out of Syracuse the next day and was at Yankee Stadium before 9 am. He checked in with Steinbrenner's secretary and sat down and waited … and waited … and waited. At 11:30 am, Lou Piniella walked by and entered the boss's office. A half-hour later, Billy Martin greeted Tex before he saw the Yankee owner. At two o'clock, Thurman Munson strolled in, talked to Tex briefly, having once been a Syracuse Chief, and then entered George's office. Finally, at 3:30 pm, Gabe Paul walked by and said, "Tex! Are you still here?" Tex upset but remaining patient, asked Paul if he could get him in to see the Yankees' owner. Paul went into Steinbrenner's office, and minutes later, Tex was sitting before the Boss.

Tex pleaded his case for the Exhibition Game, while Steinbrenner informed him that they weren't obligated to do so. Unfortunately, George was right. A major league team could provide its Triple-A affiliate with a check for $10,000 if the two sides could not agree on a date. Steinbrenner wanted to pay the fee. After an hour of persuasion, Tex got his way. George agreed to send the team to Syracuse for a 2:00 pm game on Wednesday, August 10th. Tex informed him that

Syracuse was a working person's town and that start time wouldn't work. George countered with 3:00 pm. Tex held out until Steinbrenner finally agreed to a 5:00 pm start. The Yankees were scheduled to play the Boston Red Sox the next day. A 5:00 pm start would allow the team to get to Boston from Syracuse before midnight. When the meeting concluded, George asked Tex if he wanted tickets for the Yankees game that night. "No thanks," Tex said, "I've got a 6:00 pm flight back to Syracuse and want to make it back for our game in Syracuse." Tex had won a small battle that day, but Steinbrenner's attitude convinced him that something had to change.

The game on August 10th was the same day the Chiefs were playing the Pawtucket Red Sox in the evening. The International League, sympathizing with Tex's dilemma, okayed the 5 pm game with the Yankees to be followed by Pawtucket that same evening at 8 pm. With game day approaching, ticket sales guaranteed a sellout. Then Tex got a call from Gabe Paul just days before the game. With the Yankees trailing the Red Sox in the standings, Steinbrenner preferred that his players go right to Boston and skip the Exhibition game altogether. Even if it went forward, Gabe told Tex that the Yankees would not be sending a full team. A number of players, including Munson, Sparky Lyle, Ken Holtzman, Mike Torrez, Nettles, Chambliss, and others, would skip the game.

Paul, knowing what this would mean to Tex, was able to convince his two future Hall of Famers, Reggie Jackson and Catfish Hunter, to join the diminished team so as to help out his Triple-A General Manager. At the time, there were rumors that Paul and Steinbrenner were not getting along, and possibly Paul thought that he might need Tex's support down the road. As if the loss of stars wasn't enough, a local reporter named Bud Poliquin got wind of the Yankees' plans, and he ran a story the morning of the game, letting his readers know who was not coming to Syracuse. Fortunately, Hunter, Jackson, Mickey Rivers, Cliff Johnson, Roy White, and Bucky Dent did show, so all was not lost. The team's coaching staff included Manager Billy Martin, Yogi Berra, Elston Howard, and Bobby Cox.

Hunter was currently on the disabled list and was only sched-uled to pitch in the bullpen that day. As a favor to Yankees pitching coach Cloyd Boyer, Hunter offered to come to Syracuse and help the situation. When they arrived in Syracuse, Cloyd gave Tex the good news that Catfish would start the game and pitch five innings. On the other hand, Reggie Jackson played two innings in right field and then famously walked off the field with a woman reporter.

When the game started, pitcher Grant Jackson was in left field, but center field was vacant. When someone notified Martin that his centerfielder Rivers was asleep on the trainer's table, he told the clubhouse attendant to tell Mickey that he would be fined $500 if he wasn't in centerfield immediately. After hearing Martin's threat, Rivers, clearly in no shape to play baseball that day, pulled out $500 and told the clubhouse kid to give it to Martin. With the game near its start time, that clubhouse kid did as he was told. Martin, in turn, gave the kid $100 for his efforts and sent Paul Blair out to play center field. The clubhouse kid was Tex's son, John Simone.

The game was over in less than two hours as players swung at the first hittable pitch. They were dressed and on their plane to Boston before 8:00 pm. It was the final Yankees Exhibition Game in Syracuse. It was now clear to Tex what to expect if he renewed the working agreement at the end of the season.

Meanwhile, two New York Yankees staff, Pat Gillick and Eliott Wahle, with whom Tex had a great working relationship, had been recruited by Peter Bavasi of the expansion Toronto Blue Jays to head up their development system. At Gillick's suggestion, Tex had even been invited to interview for the new position of Director of Stadium Operations in Toronto. At the time, Tex was caring for his brother Archie, who was terminally ill with colon cancer. His love for his brother outweighed any offer, and he remained in Syracuse. Pat and Elliott were keen to continue the relationship with Tex. A year later, when the Blue Jays needed an AAA team, Syracuse was their pre-ferred choice. Tex looked favorably on what might be an opportunity to support baseball's new Canadian city.

Over the years, he would take a few lumps locally for the quality of the playing talent Toronto made available during their formative years, resulting in Syracuse's absence from post-season play. Fortunately, his hands-on style as the man always available on-field and during the game elevated his local reputation. He was a visible presence to whom people could talk or vent if necessary but finally respected for his attentiveness to the needs of his community and its ball team. He knew he'd made the right choice when, after suffering at the gate in 1978 owing to the paucity of talent Toronto could send, the big league team provided the Chiefs with a $50,000 check to ensure profitability for their minor league affiliate. He knew the decision to leave the Yankees was justified, and his loyalty to the Blue Jays' organization never wavered.

On the part of the Jays, they were interested in a relationship based on player development, not winning minor league titles. As Gord Ash would explain, "We gave Tex input into his managers and coaches, but we didn't sign a lot of career minor leaguers who might have improved his situation. We had so many prospects we were developing. But there were certain players like Jerry Keller and Stu Pederson, good minor leaguers we'd sign as a designated hitter or just as an extra bat to help him."

Nor were those prospects baseball's equivalent of chopped liver. The 1991 Chiefs pitching roster coming out of spring training included Juan Guzman, who would win 30 regular season games in the Jays' two World Series winning seasons, Mike Timlin, a future bullpen ace for Toronto and Boston, and Pat Hentgen, a future Cy Young Award winner. Long-time future major leaguers included David Wells, Kelly Gruber, and Ed Sprague. Sprague spent parts of four seasons with the Chiefs and was called up for the Blue Jays' eventually successful World Series run in 1992. Dramatically, his game two home run helped turn around the Series against Atlanta.

THE PEDERSON FAMILY

During Tex's tenure, there wasn't one player and, more importantly, one family that touched him more than the Pedersons. Stu and Shelly Pederson brought their crew to Syracuse in 1988 after spending seven years playing with the Dodgers organization. He played in five games in Los Angeles in 1985 during his seven years with them. Released in spring training 1988, the Blue Jays, with the recommendation of former Dodger and now Chiefs manager Bob Bailor, signed him. He would spend the next five years with Tex and the Chiefs, building a relationship that continues today.

During his time in Syracuse, the Pederson family grew from three to five, he was part of a championship club in 1989, and he became one of the most popular players in team history. Tex recognized his popularity and decided to have a "Stu Pederson Night" in his final season. And like it was written in a script, Stu delivered with a walk-off home run in the ninth inning to win the game.

But what Tex enjoyed the most was the relationship he created with Stu, Shelly, and the kids. He always made sure Shelly had whatever she needed at games and helped her with the children when she came to the park.

He was especially fond of their first child Champ, who was a child with Down Syndrome. Champ was the most loving child you could ever meet and was loved not only by Tex but many of the fans who saw the youngster each night.

After each year, Tex would ask Shelly how much salary they needed to come back to Syracuse for the following season. He would make sure Toronto knew how important it was to sign Stu back for another year. As the years went by, it became apparent that Tex was more interested in reuniting each spring with Shelly and the kids, Champ, then Tyger and his brother Joc.

As spring training 1993 was about to begin, Toronto told Tex that they might not be able to carry his favorite family for a sixth year. Robert Perez, Rob Butler, and Willie Canate were going to dominate the playing time, and it might be time for the Pederson era to end.

He understood that it would end at some time, and Stu would begin the season at age 33, but he was still upset. So much so that he offered to pay his salary for the season. Toronto wouldn't let him do that, but Gord Ash did tell Tex he would add him to the coaching staff as the hitting instructor if he wanted.

Stu was considering the option to retire and begin a coaching career, but with three children in the fold and a burgeoning ticket broker business in California, it was time to end his career in baseball.

After his baseball career ended, Stu now managing a very successful business, often reached out to his former General Manager for help. In 1993, he asked Tex to pick up season tickets from Bills fans in Buffalo. Part of his business was to purchase season ticket holder's tickets and then turn them around and sell them to interested football fans who wanted to see a Super Bowl. The practice at a smaller level started when Stu was growing up and would be parking cars for Stanford and 49ers football games and Giants baseball games in the Bay area where he grew up. People would give him extra tickets, and the enterprising young Pederson thought, instead of going to the games, why not sell them for 100% profit? It worked. And Stu became the guy for tickets for any event on the West Coast.

As the years went by, Tex and the Pederson's would exchange Christmas cards and phone calls, and in 2012, Tex inducted his friend into the teams' Hall of Fame. A few years later, in 2017, at the Little League World Series, Champ Pederson was inducted into the LLWS Hall of Excellence, which is the highest honor Little League can bestow. While Tex had passed a few years prior to the induction, the Pederson's, especially Champ, asked that John, Tex's son, be part of the ceremony.

A year later, Champ's brother Tyger would team up with Tex's grandson Alex and help coach the Duluth Huskies Summer League team to the league championship game.

Today, Stu continues to instruct young players coaching in summer college leagues. Champ has worked for Apple and the Golden State Warriors and is an inspirational speaker.

In 2016, he unveiled a line of clothing and caps appropriately named "Live Like a Champ." His son Tyger is the minor league hitting coordinator for the Seattle Mariners. Son Joc has played 11 years in the major leagues with the Dodgers, Cubs, Braves, Giants, and Diamondbacks. He's played in four World Series, winning a championship with the Dodgers and Braves. And his daughter Jacey played soccer at UCLA.

Tex was a great man, said Pederson. He would do anything for his players and, in my case, anything for my family. He treated his players like family. I loved playing there. He made it so enjoyable and fun. What I enjoyed the most was when the public address announcer, Chris Granozio, would announce my name. Now batting Stuuuuuuuuuuuuuuuuuuuuuuuu Pederson. The fans loved it. You would hear them all join in. They even made t-shirts with my mug on the shirt and megaphones for the fans to join in. The money they raised was donated to the Special Olympics in my son Champ's name.

Moving Up Fast

In many ways, following a minor league team is like seeing a future popular band before they make it big. Imagine being a tourist in Hamburg or Liverpool in the early 1960s who caught the Beatles in their formative, pre-sensation days. Likewise, Syracuse baseball fans saw one of the National Basketball Association's notable stars, Danny Ainge, when he was still trying to make it as a third baseman with the Jays in the late 1970s and early 80s before wisely opting for the Boston Celtics' championship-winning squad.

Another stalwart was Dave Stieb, who fortunately did not have to change sports but did have to switch positions. In 1979, Jays management decided he had a future as a pitcher and not in the outfield where he had started. The transition was a huge success. He moved quickly up the ranks from Dunedin to Syracuse. Stieb went 5-2 with the Chiefs losing one game when catcher Pat Kelly threw the ball over his head, allowing the only run of the game to score.

Gillick thought he was ready for the big time. Tex called him into the Syracuse office and handed him a plane ticket to New York, where he would immediately pitch against the Yankees. Stieb questioned his readiness, but Tex reassured him, "Not only are you ready, you're the best pitcher in our League." Stieb would win 140 games for the Jays through the 1980s, second overall in the decade only to Detroit's Jack Morris.

Blue Jays Contending and Championships Years 1985-1993

In 1985, Paul Beeston had invited Tex to throw out the first pitch of game seven of the American League Championship Series against the Kansas City Royals in old Exhibition Stadium. Tex was representing all of the Blue Jays minor league personnel who had done so much to foster the team's success. Unfortunately, the Blue Jays lost that night. Baseball is a very superstitious sport, and as a result, Tex was never asked to repeat the honor. Perhaps for that reason, nobody enjoyed the Toronto Blue Jays championship years more than Tex.

Between 1985 and 1993, the Blue Jays would make the playoffs five times, with only a season-ending collapse in 1987 preventing a sixth. There were two victorious World Series years in 1992 and 1993. The Blue Jays, under Paul Beeston, made sure that the organization's affiliates and their employees shared in the success. During those years, they always invited Tex to be part of the playoff atmosphere. The pre and post-game gatherings included introductions to a galaxy of Hollywood stars, from the jovial if rotund John Candy to the dashing if taciturn Tom Selleck. Tex was in the stadium for the ultimate high point of those years when Joe Carter homered off Mitch Williams. He was covered with champagne minutes later in the Blue Jays' clubhouse, administered by many of the players who had come through Syracuse. The man who recommended dumping the World Champion New York Yankees of 1977 was now the most popular guy in Syracuse.

Tex received World Series rings for his contributions to the organization. The 1992 World Series was particularly meaningful. Not only did the Jays' lineup include 14 players who had spent time in Syracuse, but the two rivals also had personal connections with Tex. On one side was Pat Gillick, with whom his relationship dated back to the 1970s when Gillick was the New York Yankees' Director of Player Development. He had come from the Houston Astros shortly after Tal Smith made the same move. Tal was now Gabe Paul's assistant, and he had made sure Pat and Tex hit it off early. It was a remarkable relationship. It was not uncommon for Pat to call Tex at any hour of the day to get his opinion. Gillick, a noted early morning riser, often initiated a 6 am phone call to ask Tex about a player or something he'd heard the night before or to enquire how his family was. Tex loved every minute of it. On the other side was another lifelong friend and a one-time Chiefs manager, Bobby Cox, now field manager in charge of the Atlanta Braves. Both Gillick and Cox would later be inducted into baseball's Hall of Fame in Cooperstown.

The Business of Minor League Baseball

Blue Jays success didn't necessarily translate into a similar fortune for its minor league teams. Shortly after the conclusion of their last season at the Big Mac in 1996, a disgruntled Syracuse fan, Harold Berman, wrote to the local Herald Journal (11 September 1996). Berman remembered the days of former Syracuse baseball greats. "Dixie Howell never had a car. So, he would ride the bus downtown with the fans and go to his favorite restaurant. I used to hang around the baseball games, and one night, Jewel Ens, the manager of the 1947 Chiefs, finally asked me, 'Aren't you up late for a little kid?' I remember Dutch Mele and Hank Sauer being the official starters for the go-cart races that started way up on the top of Crouse Avenue and went all the way to the bottom."

All was not well with the current Chiefs, at least in Berman's analysis, "Tex has never turned down a request if he could help somebody. He is a class act, just like the stadium has been. I only wish the Toronto Blue Jays would consult with him about which players should be brought up to play in Syracuse and which players should be sent down. When you have a comfortable lead as late as July 23rd, as the Chiefs did, and you blow it through ball player trades, something is wrong. Toronto should consult Tex more. I hope the Blue Jays organization will get smart so the Chiefs can get back in the playoffs."

Mr. Berman's pleas were heartfelt but he was describing a passing world no longer in tune with baseball's new reality. This changing relationship was aptly described by Murray Cook, a one-time general manager of three major league teams: the New York Yankees (1983–84), the Montreal Expos (1984–87), and the Cincinnati Reds (1988–89). "The major/minor league affiliation has changed a lot since I started. When I started the minor league teams even owned some of their players and often sold them for a profit to a major league team – Luis Tiant being a case in point. In some ways, it's progressed or regressed since then, depending on your point of view.

"In the old days, the Triple-A team was treated as the red-headed stepchild, tolerated but not loved. For the major league team that owned their minor league affiliate, it was a money-losing proposition. In some cases, they virtually gave the team away to local owners or investors. Now, those teams are money makers largely because the major league team pays the players. The cost to the minor league affiliate can be the call-up at any time of a player regardless of the minor league team's need and position in their league at the time."

Tex knew this, and it was one over which he had input but ultimately little control. What he did control, was the status of the team in Syracuse and where they played their games. Social engagements and public speaking now became a major priority as he put in place the foundation of what would be his greatest accomplishment. Financing, building, and managing a new stadium would be the high point of his career. Without it, Minor League Baseball, at least at the Triple-A level, would forever be an uncertain proposition in Syracuse. Tex knew better than anyone that the old days in which a GM needed to be a jack of all trades, from helping the grounds crew or signing inexpensive free agents to fill out a roster before being sold on to a big team, were disappearing. Such measures had once been the difference between profit and loss. Likewise, the necessity of patching together a charming but declining facility was a strategy no longer meeting the demands of Major League Baseball.

The charms of this one-time era had given way to a new business model. Minor league teams had once been able to break even with fewer than 200,000 fans a season. Tex did this on many occasions. Now, they could be in financial jeopardy even if they drew over 300,000, as Syracuse was to do on many occasions in the new ballpark. At the same time, franchises in minor league ball, as Cook noted, had become valuable commodities pursued by more potentially robust markets themselves, often combinations of new suburban regions with names most people could not place on a map, unlike the old urban centers of the 19th century like Syracuse.

Tex with Family

Tex with friends at North High

Photo is of Tex's mother and brother

SFC Anthony M. Simone

Tex with his mother Rose

Tex at Fort Dix, NJ for basic training

Tex with his Boxing team in Stuttgart, Germany

Tex in his Baseball uniform for the Nuremberg team in Germany

Tex Playing Basketball for US Army team in Germany

Tex during his final days in Germany

Tex with his parents on his Wedding Day

Tex at the Gus Mauch Training School

Tex with Detroit Tigers Manager Bob Swift in Spring Training

Tex with Bobby Doerr

Tex with Bobby Cox (left) and Pat Gillick (right)

Tex with Cecil Fielder, Lou Thornton, Fred McGriff and Otis Green

Tex with Deion Sanders

Tex with Blue Jays General Manager Gord Ash

Tex with George M. Steinbrenner

Tex last family photo

THE NEW STADIUM

B y the 1990s, Major League Baseball was revising its expectations about the places in which its high-priced talent was being groomed for eventual success – everything from the quality of dressing rooms and the access of fans to players to safe surroundings and bullpen facilities. Syracuse's MacArthur Stadium did not rate well in these evaluations. Were it not for the extraordinary level of trust between Tex Simone and the Toronto Blue Jays' management team, a decision to abandon Syracuse might have been easy. Instead, the Blue Jays rallied to Tex's cause proclaiming by their regular visits to Syracuse their interest in maintaining this extraordinary relationship. Tex's challenge was not his major league partner but finding a way to get enough financial support from some combination of Onondaga County, the city of Syracuse, private interests, and even the state government. Besides financing, location would prove to be just as big of a challenge, in some ways a trickier one.

Financing, Construction and Management

Thinking about a new stadium began almost from the time of MacArthur Stadium's necessary restoration in the years following the disastrous fire of 1969. As early as 1979, Tex was telling visiting groups of fans about the need for artificial turf either in MacArthur or a new facility. He would be the driving force behind these first conversations about a new facility. Next, he was wrestling with sources of funding and the location of such a facility. Finally, he would oversee the construction process and the management of the new facility's expanded range of events and obligations.

In 1987, Chiefs President Don Waful appointed a committee to study the rehabilitation of MacArthur. By spring of the next year, there was general agreement on the need for a multipurpose facility in which not only baseball but also outdoor concerts, other sports, and high school activities would be possible. In the summer of 1989, the Chiefs and Onondaga County studied prospects for the expansion of the existing stadium. Noted ballpark designers HOK were hired to put a price tag on the project. By 1991, MacArthur's limitations, even for a significant upgrade, had become increasingly apparent.

Reluctantly for some, necessary in the eyes of others, plans were unveiled for a new multi-purpose facility next door to MacArthur. Officials at the state government of New York were lobbied for financial help. Around the same time, Major League Baseball said MacArthur no longer met its minimal functional requirements. The State of New York pitched an $800 million Jobs Bond Act, part of which would be used for the funding of new stadiums in the state, but the act was voted down in the fall elections.

Fortunately, that was not the end of the conversation. The Blue Jays kept the pursuit alive by committing $1 million for the stadium turf, as well as guaranteeing a loan of $4 million taken out by the Chiefs towards the overall project. At the State level, Governor Mario Cuomo was committed to looking for alternative ways his government could participate in the planning and financing of new or upgraded stadiums State-wide. New York State Assemblyman and Board member Hy Miller and Tex's best friend Armand Magnarelli, himself a local politician, were instrumental in convincing Governor Cuomo.

At the same time, a debate raged through the summer of 1993 on a downtown location versus a building near MacArthur Stadium off Hiawatha Boulevard. Tex was committed to the same location, one he had known since his childhood. It was a place to which he had made the several mile trek climbing a hill from his north Syracuse home. Opened in 1934 as Municipal Stadium, its name was later changed to salute the Second World War hero of the Pacific, General Douglas MacArthur, by which time its 10,000-seat capacity had lots of room in which Tex and his teenage buddies could roam.

Sixty years after its opening, a local preference was emerging favoring Syracuse's downtown, where it might have city-building potential as either an enhancement of or inducement for more public transit, urban amenities, restaurants, and bars. It had become the preferred option for many new ballparks throughout the United States. Baltimore's Camden Yards and Buffalo's new Pilot Field were two contemporary examples.

The success of such ballparks depended on the foundation of a vibrant downtown with lots of people living, working, and being entertained within walking distance. Without such character, it would be little more than a place to which fans commuted in cars, spent considerable time looking for parking, and left the city as soon as the game was over. To this day, Buffalo's downtown ballpark remains largely a commuter site from which finding a taxi or walking with others to nearby residences after the game is not possible. It's not because it is dangerous but because so few live nearby, and there is no reasonable business case for a taxi owner to linger in the hope of passengers.

Tex favored the predictability of the current site. While also dependent on people driving to the game, they could be assured of a parking spot next to the ballpark. It had been good enough for sixty years; why not another sixty? A new factor arose in a nearby wetlands site described as having once been part of a rare inland salt marsh. Questions remained as to its current quality and whether, if it was not in good health, it could be regenerated with the potentially prohibitive cost of doing so. The uniqueness of its salt marshes in the 19th century meant Syracuse was at one time the only American city producing salt commercially, for which it had been quaintly dubbed the Salt City.

Meanwhile, the cost of land acquisition for a downtown ballpark site near Armory Square was going to add several million dollars to the final cost. Current neighboring uses, not conducive to the spin-off benefits of a downtown park, questioned the impact of a new stadium on their current operation.

Tex remained committed to the existing location even when a newspaper cartoonist suggested his attitude was comparable to that of a small boy who demands his friends play his game or else he'll take his bat and ball and go home. The Chiefs, led by Tex, eventually won their fight for the present north side locale. Next, the Governor came through with State funding for sports facilities, of which $14 million was dedicated to the Syracuse project. In 1994, HOK began work on the design of the new multipurpose stadium. Later in the summer, County lawmakers approved $3 million as their contribution to the new stadium. There was brief panic early in 1995 when stadium funding was missing from the state budget, but a few months later, $16 million was returned for this purpose, and the facility was targeted for opening in April 1997. Around the same time, the Chiefs signed a 15-year lease with the county.

The first bid packages went out in June. The driving of steel piles followed soon after. Tex Simone smashed a bottle of champagne against those piles in September as if he were commissioning a new ship. Concrete slab-pouring followed before interior work, including masonry, plumbing, electricity, sprinkler mains, and branches (particularly appropriate given the old stadium's fate in 1969). Exterior brickwork followed giving the stadium its distinctive heritage feel. Parking lot paving followed in September, as well as the shock pad for artificial turf installation.

The last game was played in MacArthur in September 1996. Terry McGriff grounded out to end the ballpark's history. Less than a year later, the new stadium opened to rave reviews as spectators entered the grounds along the aptly named Tex Simone Drive. No sooner had the new stadium become a reality were questions raised about who would manage it beyond its use for baseball. The installation of an artificial turf surface now facilitated other sporting events, from lacrosse and soccer to high school football and perhaps even field hockey, as well as concerts and special events not suitable for an arena.

There were suggestions Tex and his staff were not up to the challenges of marketing a Triple-A ball club now about to be housed in a high-end minor league stadium. It was an acceptable arrangement, critics argued, when Tex's management team made the best of the reduced public expectations associated with a declining MacArthur Stadium. A new park with modern amenities and in the model, if not the capacity, of its more recent major league counterparts required a different approach. "In a nutshell," *Post-Standard* reporter Matt Michael said, "They wondered if Mom and Pop could handle the move to a chain store."

Tex responded to the criticism, "Who can handle this if we can't? It amazes me. We turned a $27,000 investment into a franchise valued at $8 million right now. Toronto has confidence in our ability to market and manage this thing. They wouldn't have given us a $1 million gift and guaranteed our $4 million loan if they didn't. We've been successful since 1970, so evidently, we're doing something right." In such a climate, the Chiefs required a wise voice at the top of its management structure to interpret the new baseball reality and to navigate its challenging shoals. Tex stepped up to the position of executive vice president and chief operating officer, while John Simone took on the full-time General Manager role.

Changes in Blue Jays Leadership

After Pat Gillick left the Jays following the 1994 season, Tex had to recalibrate his relationship with the big team. Gillick was a good friend, but Tex had created an equally strong relationship with Paul Beeston. He had also supported, mentored in some ways, Gillick's replacement, Gord Ash. Gillick's departure coincided with the Jays decline from their championship seasons. In retrospect, Tex wasn't completely surprised, but at the same time, he welcomed Gord Ash's enthusiastic appreciation for what was, after all, only the mid-point in the 31-year affiliate relationship.

"I'd known of Tex from when he came up to Toronto for meetings," Ash recalled. "Everyone spoke highly of him. As I got to know Tex more directly, I discovered what a treat it was to work with him. He was an old-school operator who knew the importance of keeping expenses down at the minor-league level. He got a lot of ribbing for being thrifty; as an example he had his own ball cleaning device, something like you might see on a golf course, for ensuring a ball could be used again. He dried out waterlogged balls and some of them weren't seconds or thirds either but perhaps in their eighth or ninth use. If he had to pull tarp to protect a game from cancellation, he did. If an usher didn't show up, he'd help people find their seats. He'd even take tickets if required. I understood his situation perfectly because I'd done so many of those things myself as I was advancing through the Jays' organization.

"We knew it had been difficult for Syracuse to leave the Yankees, but Tex came to relish the relationship with the Jays. He never complained about call-ups. For our part, we were aware of his situation. We tried to leave his lineup intact by not moving guys back and forth between Toronto and Syracuse. He knew how the major-minor league affiliation worked. He was one of the first minor league operators to realize that at that level, you had to market the team for the fun of a day or evening out. Wins and losses were something you didn't have a lot of control over.

"Interestingly though, the Blue Jays now have an affiliation with Buffalo, that wouldn't have worked back in the 80s and 90s. Buffalo's interest in those days was in putting a winning team on the field, while ours was player development. Still, we sent some really good players through Syracuse – Roy Halliday, Vernon Wells, Tony Fernandez, Chris Carpenter, Carlos Delgado, Lloyd Moseby, and others. Only Barfield and Olerud missed playing there."

Ash left the Blue Jays after 2001 and had a long career with the Milwaukee Brewers, but he remains sensitive to the role of a minor league team, its location, and even its league plays in the success of the major league organization.

"I would go to Syracuse two or three times a season and it wasn't just to put in an appearance and leave. I'd meet with Tex or John in the morning, discuss their situation and ours, we'd go for lunch, and then I'd stay for the game. It was part of the process, keeping us there for 31 years. After I left, someone from the Jays rarely came down. It played a role in Syracuse eventually looking for another affiliate. I saw the same thing in Milwaukee. We didn't always have the best relationship with our minor league affiliate be it in Indianapolis or Nashville, but I argue the right location of your minor league team matters. It's best if it's within driving distance. For the Jays, being in the International League was a huge advantage. Guys going down might not be quick to get there, but going the other way to the majors, it was important a player be able to get to Toronto, particularly if you needed him for that night's game. In the International League, you don't have the altitude or time difference issues you have with a team in the west like Colorado Springs or Las Vegas."

Having let Gord Ash go after the 2001 season, the Blue Jays and their new management team expressed an interest in going in a different direction. Under Club President Paul Godfrey, and particularly new General Manager J.P. Ricciardi, the Blue Jays paid greater attention to the club's bottom line and also to the emerging analytics approach as eventually celebrated in Michael Lewis's 2003 book *Moneyball: The Art of Winning an Unfair Game.* It was dubbed sabermetrics for the manner in which members of the Society for American Baseball Research (SABR) helped pioneer the study of baseball statistics as a tool for measuring in-game activity and undervalued talent.

For his part, Ricciardi favored college players over high school prospects. It had several implications. For one, and at least in theory, it meant such players were further along in the development process, with a reduced amount of minor league time required. Being somewhat older meant their ultimate potential was easier to scope. Finally, it often meant a decided overabundance of white middle-class prospects more likely to go the college route, as opposed to Dominican and other island ballplayers or those from African-American inner-city neighborhoods, the latter already a declining total of the major league's overall demographic profile.

This would eventually be a controversial topic in the Toronto media, but its emergence appeared unintentional at least from being a conscious decision to forgo minority players. It was an inevitable result of a policy placing those minority and off-shore candidates in a somewhat more precarious position when it came to their evaluation. For Syracuse and other minor league teams in the Jays' system, as well as for its long-respected scouting system, the result was a diminishing significance. When Ricciardi was first introduced to Tex by the one-time Blue Jays field manager Bobby Mattick, it was with the words, "JP, this is Tex Simone. He's the best GM in baseball, and we have been with him since 1978. Don't screw it up".

For many of the reasons described above, Toronto went in another direction. It took time, but eight years later, the Blue Jays era would end in part because there was also mounting pressure from the Syracuse Chiefs' Board of Directors to look for a new affiliate.

TEX BATTLES
OTHER ODDS

John Simone remembers the day like it was yesterday, "It was Sunday, February 4, 1987, and my mother called to say Dad was not feeling well. When I got to their house, he was waiting at the door to go to the hospital. We went to St. Joseph's, just minutes from where he grew up. Within minutes, the ER Staff told me he was having a heart attack. The next 24 hours were touch and go. His doctor, who was also the team's physician and a long-time friend, Dr. Armand Cincotta, told me he might not make it. Dad was a four-cups-of-coffee-a-day drinker, but more deadly were the two, sometimes three packs, of Kent cigarettes he smoked every day, at least in part, because of the daily stress of running all aspects of the baseball operation. He had started smoking in his neighborhood when he was only ten and was temporarily suspended from the baseball team by his coach, Arlo Bush, when he was caught. Forty-six years later, at the age of 56, it had finally caught up to him."

Tex survived. It was diagnosed as a stress heart attack. Combined with his smoking and a diet of many Italian meals, it was not a good recipe for one's arteries. He came home a few weeks later with orders to change his diet and stop smoking. He would spend the next three months at home. With opening day 1987 just six weeks away, it would mean he would miss his first Home Opener in quite a while. The day he left the hospital with his family, he put on his coat, and in its pocket, he pulled out a pack of cigarettes and looked at them and then at his son John. John asked, "What are you going to do with them?" Tex tossed them in the garbage, and the two of them left. He never smoked again.

It was a rough late winter and early spring for Tex, one to which he was not familiar. He enlisted friends, relatives, and everyone except those of his immediate family to sneak him down to the ballpark to see what was happening. They would drop him off at the stadium maintenance building located down the right-field line. He sat in the office overlooking the stadium. As long as he remained there, the family turned a blind eye. As Opening Day approached, the team, as was the annual custom, selected someone to toss out the first pitch. In 1987, it was a no-brainer: Tex.

"To keep him from arguing with us about the choice, we waited until game day to tell him," John says. "There was a crowd of over 7,000 fans on a beautiful 70-degree day, and Tex walked out to the mound, where he had been thousands of times before. But this time, he was by himself. And after he was announced and the crowd gave him a standing ovation he tossed a perfect strike to Chiefs catcher Greg Meyers. He was officially back."

Lifestyle changes followed his return to work – no coffee or cigarettes. His diet of chicken, turkey and all things healthy dominated his life going forward. Five years later, Tex was healthy and feeling great until a yearly checkup showed that he had cancer in his colon. It was the same thing that 15 years before had befallen his oldest brother Archie, to whom he'd sent all those letters during his armed forces days. It had been too late to save Archie, who died at 62, the same age Tex had now reached. Fortunately, Tex's cancer was detected early enough, but he would lose 12 inches of colon.

It was quite a one-two punch, but more was to come. In 1996, adding to the stress of building a new stadium, Tex began to experience throat pain. No cancer was detected, but he periodically had his throat scraped for possible polyps. Eventually, throat cancer was discovered in 2005. Surgery was required to remove his vocal cords. Losing his voice was daunting for a man who spent his entire life communicating. Ultimately, Tex would be largely silent for the rest of his life. The surgery was undertaken, appropriately enough, during the off-season in November 2005. It was a success, but for a 76-year-old man, these health issues were taking a toll. He would miss his first Baseball Winter Meetings held in Dallas, a streak going back to 1969 in Fort Lauderdale when Tony Henninger, the city's one-time mayor and now banker, paid for his trip; the team then on financially shaky ground and unable to afford it.

The family and Chiefs staff adjusted to Tex's new means of communication, but he would soon be overtaken by the early onset of Alzheimer's. He lost his license briefly in 2006 after a car accident and relied on the kindness of family members to drive him around town. While this was all happening, Tex began to follow a daily routine characteristic for those with the disease. He would have notes on his desk. They helped him remember the names of the people in his office, his grandchildren, and even what he would eat on certain days of the week. He hid his memory loss as well as could be expected as the years went by. Family and friends made sure to protect him and help him along the way.

BROADCASTING

Broadcasting a Minor League Baseball team's games on the radio continued to be an important aspect of their necessary promotion. Tex took it seriously. Growing up he had spent many nights listening to radio broadcasts of major league games called by the likes of Mel Allen, Red Barber, and Ernie Harwell. When he went to spring training with the New York Mets in the early 1960s, he got to meet the broadcast crew of Lindsey Nelson, Bob Murphy, and Ralph Kiner. Later, he became great friends with the immortal voice of the Detroit Tigers, Ernie Harwell, and later with Yankees announcers Phil Rizzuto, Jerry Coleman, Joe Garagiola, Frank Messer, and Bill White. Finally, he befriended the Blue Jays' Tom Cheek and Jerry Howarth.

As a trainer his dealings with the team's radio announcers were about ensuring they received the club's itinerary and meal money. Once he moved to the front office he was directly involved in managing the team's radio broadcasts as they often rotated through various stations in the community. With the exception of one season, the team's voice between 1966 and 1979 was John Harmon. He was from Birmingham, Alabama where he had been part of the Alabama Football broadcast team in the 1960s when Bear Bryant was there. He began his minor-league career broadcasting for the Birmingham Barons at old Rickford Field in the Southern League, then moved on to the Richmond Virginians in the International League before spending the bulk of his career in Syracuse. Tex would spend many nights on the road eating dinner with the southerner who regaled him with events from his storied career.

As General Manager, Tex made sure John was the team's broadcaster and thus part of the championship teams in 1969, 1970, and 1976. Before the start of the 1976 season, a new station manager told Tex they wanted to replace Harmon with a rising young local television broadcaster, Tom Pipines. The station manager said it was Pipines or no broadcast.

The season was just weeks away, and so Harmon was left without a team. Tex showed the compassion he had for his friends and employees. He helped John supplement his lost income by getting the local newspapers to hire him as their stringer. John wrote game stories for the Associated Press and he assumed official scorer duties at all home games. Tex made sure John's living quarters were paid for and invited him for dinner at least once a week. While the 1976 season was a success on the field, with the team capturing their seventh Governor's Cup Championship, the removal of Harmon from the broadcast booth bothered Tex.

In 1977, Pipines parlayed his experience with the Chiefs into joining the fledging new sports channel ESPN and spent four years there before moving to Milwaukee to announce for the NBA Bucks and Marquette University. With Pipines gone and the station's general manager as well, Tex was able to bring Harmon back for three more years until the 1980 season. Sensing the team's only option might be moving to a student-run radio station at Syracuse University, Tex arranged for Harmon to hook up with the Rochester Red Wings for the next few seasons before his eventual retirement. Syracuse University's Newhouse School of Communications had graduated the likes of Ted Koppel, Dick Stockton, Marv Albert, Bob Costas, Joe Castiglione, Andy Musser, Dick Clark, and Marty Glickman, to name a few. The University was keen on providing a great training ground for its students. Tex saw this as a way to keep fans up to date with Chiefs Baseball on the radio.

During the next four-year period, some wonderful young broadcasters got their start in the radio booth high above MacArthur Stadium. They included Bob Black and Bob Licht and were followed by Sean McDonough, John Stashower, Greg Papa, and later Craig Minervini, Mike Tirico, and others. All of those young men went on to broadcast in minor league, major league, and network television during their careers and were appreciative of the opportunities that the relationship provided.

Sean McDonough's father, Will, was a Boston Globe sportswriter and later an insider reporter for the NFL on CBS and NBC. The younger McDonough became friends with Tex's son John. Tex would often invite Sean over for dinner, and he, too, became close to the aspiring young broadcaster. Tex had some concerns about Sean's intentions when the latter invited the Syracuse GM to the Newhouse School to speak at one of his classes. The student-run station on campus, WAER-88.3 FM, was considering hiring professional talent to run their operation, thus freezing out the students who had run it for over 20 years. When Tex arrived, he saw all three television stations and their trucks. When he entered the building, he noticed a number of students with signs, and before he could read what they said, there was Sean McDonough standing on a table in the cafeteria yelling through a megaphone, "Down with the chancellor!" Tex realized he had been invited to a student revolt aimed at the Dean of the Newhouse School and the Chancellor of the University. Tex quickly exited the building.

Later in the year, despite this unwelcome surprise, Tex had an opportunity to help Sean. Every year, the campus station selects a student as Sports Director. This year, it was Greg Papa. As was the custom, he would present Tex with a list of broadcasters available to work that summer. It was apparent that Papa and McDonough were not getting along. After another disagreement, Papa decided to remove McDonough from the broadcast. He called Tex to advise him. In his fatherly way Tex told Papa that while he respected his authority as the station's sports director, he didn't decide on who broadcasts Chiefs games. He invited Papa and McDonough into his office to patch up their differences. Papa would later go on to broadcast in the National Football League for the Raiders and 49ers, Major League

Baseball for the Athletics and Giants, and in the National Basketball Association for the Pacers, Spurs, and Warriors.

In 1984, Syracuse University was wavering on whether to continue with the Chiefs for another year despite using the minor league broadcasts as a recruiting incentive for attracting students. Tex, in turn, now had an opportunity to return to a commercial broadcaster. The Chiefs opted for WFBL. They brought with them a young Sean McDonough, who had graduated from Syracuse University the season before. McDonough lasted only one season before moving on to his native Boston and working for NESN, becoming the television voice of the Boston Red Sox.

Over the next 30 years, Dan Hoard (Cincinnati Bengals), Doug Sherman (ESPN), Matt Vasgersian (MLB Network), Bob McElligott (Columbus Blue Jackets), Jason Benetti (Chicago White Sox & ESPN), Mike Couzens (ESPN), and Kevin Brown (Baltimore Orioles and ESPN) called games for the team. Tex was proud of the young people he helped get started, and they, in turn, appreciated the opportunity he and the team had given them.

Sean McDonough had broadcast Chiefs games between 1982 and 1984. He said of Tex, "When I first met him, I thought he had a gruff exterior; I wondered, did this guy even like me? Over time, I came to realize he cared about you ... he cared about you a lot." A few years later, as CBS's national broadcasting voice, he called not one but two memorable World Series victories by the Chiefs major league affiliate. For the first, he said, "Nixon bunts! Timlin on it! Throws to the first ... For the first time in history, the world championship banner will fly north of the border. The Toronto Blue Jays are baseball's best in 1992." The next year, he followed with, "Well-hit down the left-field line! Way back and GONE! Joe Carter with a three-run homer. The winners and still world champions, the Toronto Blue Jays."

While broadcasting in the early 1990s, Doug Sherman, a Syracuse University product and local announcer from nearby Chittenango, NY, was dating a young woman, Carolyn (CJ) Silas, who appeared as a regular in the person of Laura Mackie in season six of the TV series

Fame that ran from 1982-87. She was from Los Angeles but had decided to transfer from the University of Southern California (USC), where she was studying drama, to Syracuse University's Newhouse School of Communications in 1992. CJ was also interested in making the transfer from acting to sports broadcasting and told Tex she'd like to apply for the Chiefs' Public Address Announcer position. "You know we have never had a woman PA announcer," Tex said, but CJ told him, "All the more reason to hire me." Tex did, and the PA announcements at old MacArthur Stadium broke another barrier. She went on to work for ESPN in Bristol, Connecticut, after graduation and has since worked as a syndicated talk show host for the past 30 years on CBS Sportsline and ESPN Radio and played in the Cal Skate Roller Derby League.

In the winter of 1988, as was the case every year, Tex received letters and tapes from aspiring young broadcasters. Tex was set for the upcoming season, with Dan Hoard beginning his fourth season. However, this letter was unlike any other he had received. It came from a fellow in California. He was out of work but looking to do something for which he had always aspired – broadcasting Minor League Baseball. He was Ken Levine, a successful Hollywood writer with credits including *M*A*S*H, Cheers, Frasier, The Simpsons, Wings, Everybody Loves Raymond, Becker,* and *Dharma and Greg.* The screenwriters guild was going on strike that winter, and Levine figured now was the time to fulfill his dream. Tex met with him a few weeks later and Levine joined Hoard for the 1988 season.

Ken Levine's 1988 broadcasting season in Syracuse left him with fond memories. He would later create a character, Antoine "Tex" O'Hara, owner of the fictional Springfield Isotopes for *The Simpsons*. It was a memorable tip of the hat to his one-time mentor, Tex Simone. On his website, Levine recalled his season in Syracuse, "Our station had a weaker signal than my home WiFi transmitter has today," he says, no doubt somewhat tongue in cheek. "At night, you couldn't hear it at the ballpark. When people complained, I used to say that this was just the flagship station of the Worldwide Syracuse Chiefs

Radio Network. I would pause for station identification every half hour and make up all this crap about how popular the Chiefs were in Nepal and Bhutan."

A few years later, Dan Hoard became sports director for a local television station, and the team needed a new voice. They turned to Matt Vasgersian, who had spent the previous four years at places like Huntington, West Virginia; High Desert, California; and El Paso, Texas. Vasgersian had grown up in a family of entertainers. He was a child actor in the 1980s, appearing in *The Streets of San Francisco* television show and the movie ***The Candidate***. He was talented, and when Minor League Baseball introduced a weekly "Minor League Game of the Week" in 1995, they wanted Vasgersian to be their play-by-play announcer. Tex, realizing that this would be a great opportunity for the 28-year-old, allowed him to leave the team each week to travel around the minor league circuit. His time in Syracuse was short, leaving at the end of the season to return to the West Coast for a position with the Tucson Toros of the Pacific Coast League. A year later, he became the voice of the Milwaukee Brewers, then moved on to the San Diego Padres before joining the MLB Network.

MOVING IN ANOTHER DIRECTION

I n 2006, a Syracuse news report described internal board discussions in which it was proposed to jettison the Blue Jays' affiliation for one with either the Yankees or the Mets. Uncertainty as to those possibilities, as well as respect for a 29-year relationship with Toronto, among the longest in the minors, resulted in a two-year extension. As an end loomed with the Blue Jays' affiliation in 2008, a weakened Tex Simone, now beset by the challenges to his aging body, argued for its continuance. In a last-minute phone call, Tex pleaded with Blue Jays management to come to Syracuse and talk to the board. He was told the team had an important series that weekend against Boston, and no one was available. It all but sealed the deal. The Chiefs had left the Yankees many years before because owner Steinbrenner failed to put in an appearance; now, the Blue Jays, under new leadership, were committing a similar sin of neglect. Compounding the decision was the inability of Director of Player Development Dick Scott to put a winning team in Syracuse. It had been a failure not unique to this relationship but was now the proverbial last straw of disaffection.

The Board of Directors made it known to Tex and John that they wanted to explore other options for the 2009 season. Some Board members either had not been around or had simply forgotten how Toronto played such a key role in getting the new stadium built by providing guarantees for a four million dollar loan and a one million dollar gift. These measures helped keep baseball in Syracuse and able to retain its community-ownership structure. The Board wanted an affiliation with the New York Mets and directed the Simones to make it happen. While rules prohibited teams from contacting each other while still engaged with another affiliate, transgression was common. In the summer of 2008, Tex had let Toronto and Dick Scott know that it would be very difficult to sign another deal. Attempts by the Blue Jays to re-up were instead met with a non-committal Board saying it wanted to wait until season end before making a decision. Another losing season helped cement their decision.

During the summer, Tex enlisted the support of his friend Michael J. Bragman, who a few years prior was a New York State Assemblyman, a prominent Democrat, and good friends with Senator Charles Schumer. The Mets' Triple-A affiliate was in Las Vegas, and a move east made a lot of sense. Bragman arranged for Schumer, on his way from Albany to Buffalo, to meet Tex at the Syracuse airport to explore the idea. Schumer agreed to contact Fred Wilpon, owner of the Mets, to inform them Syracuse would likely not re-sign with Toronto and they would be open to an offer from the Mets. Years before, in the early 1980s, Fred Wilpon had asked if Tex could find a place for his son Jeff on the Syracuse Junior Chiefs' summer league team. Tex made it happen. The junior team even played their games at MacArthur Stadium when the Minor League Chiefs were on the road. Fred Wilpon appreciated the gesture. Around this time, Tex got wind that the Buffalo franchise was not pleased with the Cleveland Indians and was also pursuing the Mets. Buffalo owners Bob and Mindy Rich were good friends of the Wilpons.

Schumer informed Tex that Buffalo was a more likely landing spot for the Mets franchise. When Tex did talk to Jeff Wilpon at 12:01 pm on September 14, 2008, the first day you could talk to a major league club, the younger Wilpon thanked Tex for his support back when he was playing and discussed the possibility of them working to-gether. But there was a catch. Wilpon told Tex the Mets would only be interested in an agreement if they were able to purchase a majority interest in the team. It was a huge ask from a community-owned team, and one Tex could not have accomplished overnight. Like omens in a Shakespearean play, it foretold Syracuse's eventual fate.

A few days later, the Mets announced that they would be going to Buffalo. At the press conference, Senator Schumer welcomed the Mets' organization to Western New York. Tex still had held out hope for a Blue Jays reunion until a visit by the Washington Nationals and their owner Mark Lerner, General Manager Jim Bowden, Assistant General Manager Mike Rizzo, and other staff swept the Board off its feet. Syracuse Chiefs became the Triple-A affiliate of the Washington Nationals, ironically the direct franchise descendants of the Montreal Expos, the very city whose own Minor League franchise Syracuse had assumed a half-century before. It was not a bad second choice. The Nationals would send some of their brightest prospects here. Pitcher Steven Strasburg once drew a record crowd of nearly 14,000 fans. Bryce Harper made a brief 2012 stop in Syracuse.

Stephen Strasburg Experience

When the Chiefs switched affiliations after the 2008 season from Toronto to the Washington Nationals, there was an almost immediate bonus. Stephen Strasburg was selected by the Nationals, but he would not pitch in 2009 as contract negotiations with his agent, Scott Boras, dragged on until the end of the season. The Nationals sent him to their spring training site in September with the hopes of starting his career in spring training 2010. By next March, Tex Simone had made his way to the Nationals' spring training site. Tex's professional baseball career included up-close observations of Denny McLain, Mickey Lolich, John Hiller from his Tiger years, Stan Bahnsen, Ron Guidry, and Scott McGregor from his Yankee days, and then many great arms during the 31 years with the Blue Jays including Dave Stieb, Jimmy Key, David Wells, Todd Stottlemyre, Chris Carpenter, Roy Halladay, and Tom Henke. Could this guy be any better?

Strasburg made his first start in early March in Viera, Florida, and Tex witnessed it sitting next to Nationals owner Mark Lerner and his

GM Mike Rizzo. While impressed with his arm and make-up, Tex was also interested in what the crowd size might be that day. A little over 7,000 showed up that afternoon to see the phenom, a 2,000 or 3,000 bump on a regular game. The Nationals would later announce that spring that Strasburg would start the 2010 season at AA-Harrisburg, and he would eventually progress through the organization including AAA-Syracuse.

Nationals Pitching Coordinator Stan Williams was in charge of Strasburg that spring and had begun to consider when he would make his Syracuse debut. Williams pitched 14 years in the major leagues, mostly with the Dodgers, and even met Tex towards the end of his career when he pitched for Pawtucket. He would later spend time in the major leagues as a pitching coach before joining the Nationals in 2010. It was important to the Nationals GM Mike Rizzo to manage Strasburg's starts around the home schedule of their affiliates. Williams was in charge of making that happen.

Strasburg made five starts for Harrisburg before Rizzo personally called Tex in late April to tell him that the young phenom would be a Syracuse Chief. Get ready! Tex was monitoring the attendance numbers for his starts, and while the crowds were larger than normal for early April games in the Eastern League, nothing would prepare him for what was about to happen. The phenom was to arrive on an off day as the Chiefs returned from a road trip. He would meet the staff and get ready to pitch a few days later. Tex was told he was driving up from Harrisburg with his wife, and they would stop at the stadium to meet everyone.

There was a buzz of anticipation throughout the community, the media, and the front office. As everyone left for lunch, Tex was left in the office by himself. A young California native strolled down the hallway looking for someone to whom he might introduce himself. Finally, he knocked on Tex's door and said, "Are you Mr. Simone?" Tex said, "Yes, I am; how can I help you?" He said, "I'm Stephen Strasburg. I was told to come in and introduce myself." That impressed Tex, who had dealt with everyone from Casey Stengel to Deion Sanders during his long career. "I always appreciated a player who was humble, and Stephen Strasburg initially impressed me with his humility."

His first start was scheduled for a few days later, on May 8th, against the Toledo Mud Hens. Those days were filled with media requests from all over the country. The ticket office had not seen this volume of sales since the day the stadium opened in 1997. 13,766 showed up that first night, including political leaders, fans from DC, and even Syracuse University's acclaimed basketball coach, Jim Boeheim, and his family. With a record-setting crowd arriving, everyone was on deck. Tex helped park cars. The Washington Nationals' President Stan Kasten stopped and asked Tex, obviously tongue in cheek. "What's the fuss? Is something special happening tonight?" Tex made sure the Nationals' President was able to park five feet from the stadium entrance and then escorted him inside to show him the spectacle that was Stephen Strasburg. No player had ever brought out crowds of this size. There would be three more crowds of 14,000 adding to his legacy before an eventual call-up to Washington in early June.

Along the way, there were a few bumps and bruises. The minor league uniform contract that even Strasburg had to sign allowed the team he was playing for to use his likeness while he was in uniform. His agent, Scott Boras, one of the most high-profile agents in sports, objected to the team profiting off the sale of Strasburg jerseys and merchandise. Boras, who had played in the minor leagues in the 1970s, understood what Strasburg's stay in Syracuse meant to a minor league franchise, but he decided to cause problems for the team. After his playing career had ended, Boras became a player agent. Mike Fischlin and Bill Caudill were his first clients. Fischlin's connection to Tex was as a minor leaguer signed by Pat Gillick back in 1975. Fischlin was playing in AA-West Haven when he was sent to the Astros in a trade for Cliff Johnson. After his playing career, he managed for the Blue Jays organization in A-Myrtle Beach before joining his friend Scott Boras in the early 1990s. Fischlin would often visit Syracuse and bring Boras along with him. Some 30 years later, Boras would challenge Tex and the Chiefs over his client's merchandising rights.

The Boras group contacted the International League President, Randy Mobley, and Nationals President, Stan Kasten, who were told that the Syracuse Club needed to cease all sales of Strasburg merchandise. Mobley and Kasten told Boras, "You call Tex and tell him. We aren't." Boras then had one of his assistants call the Chiefs' office and tell Tex the bad news. Tex's reply, "You tell Scott Boras to call me himself. Otherwise, it's not happening. This is our one opportunity, and we own his rights." Boras called back a day later and, after conferring with the Nationals and the International League, decided that Tex could sell Strasburg's likeness. But going forward the uniform players' contract was changed to reflect what Boras was after. It didn't matter to Tex; he knew Strasburg would never be back in the minor leagues.

A year later, the Nationals again finished with the worst record in baseball and had the luck to draft their second phenom in three years – an 18-year-old outfielder named Bryce Harper. While progression for the 18-year-old was thought to be quicker than normal, no one imagined he would arrive in Syracuse in 2012. He was sent to Syracuse near the end of the Nationals 2012 spring camp. While the thought of Strasburg 2.0 with Harper was considered, it never materialized, and the now 19-year-old would play in only 21 games with the Chiefs, never attracting a crowd of more than 2,000 fans. Harper was no Strasburg. And Tex knew that might never happen ever again.

PROBLEMS IN SYRACUSE

But all was not clearly well with the Syracuse community-owned business model. In 2011, entrepreneur Arthur Solomon, owner of two other lower-level minor league teams, enquired about purchasing the Chiefs, now sporting their old familiar name. At the time, John Simone said, "Usually, we tell them about our community-owned set-up with a Board of Directors representing 16,000 stockholders, none of whom can vote more than 500 shares regardless of how many shares they own. We never hear from them again." However, Solomon's request had been supported by two directors at the time whose motivation foretold later events and the financial windfall available if the team was eventually privatized. Within a few years, such voting share restrictions could not hold back the tide of increased interest in owning a piece of the team, particularly owing to financial losses accruing from the combined bad fortune of inclement weather, competing entertainment interests in the city and region, and the team's poor performance on the field.

THE END

For many years, Tex could rely on support and continuity from three main allies. One was his general health. Other than a few bumps in the road, his commanding presence was as the face of the Syracuse Chiefs. Not for nothing would Paul Beeston say, "Tex Simone **was** the Syracuse Chiefs."

A second was the long-running 31-year affiliation with the major league Toronto Blue Jays. They gave Tex a powerful external supporter. World Series victories in '92 and '93 added to the strength of the relationship, as did their financial backing for the team's new stadium. The long-time Blue Jays association would become less robust over time as its main supporters, first Pat Gillick, then Paul Beeston (though he would later return), and finally, Gord Ash, left the organization. Voices in Syracuse, once muffled by Tex's dominant persona as the affiliate's proponent, were increasingly loud in their demand for a winning team despite the minor league team's primary role as the developer of talent.

Most significant was a changing view of the Chiefs' community-ownership model. It had relied on a Board of Directors acting in the role of stewards of a public trust. New leadership, in some cases descendants of the team's original stewards, had a different perspective on what was required for Syracuse's future success. The team's ownership structure limited the number of shares with voting power. It prevented anyone compiling enough to benefit from the franchise's accrual in value thus allowing them to sell the team to the highest bidder with no commitment to remaining in Syracuse.

The challenges surrounding these bumps were not lost on Tex, as stated in his words: "I think I have learned more about what David felt like when he was looking up at Goliath. I've learned a lesson that there are those who are involved with the county political scene and those with the newsprint business who will try to do anything to change our board and leadership, which has been very successful over the many years. I've learned it can get pretty personal and brutal when they get together to accomplish their goal. I've put my life into professional baseball and gave my heart and soul to keep it here in Syracuse and to help make it successful."

As long as the team met its bottom line obligations and was run in a manner contributing to the overall health, safety, and the good name of Syracuse, the model had proved fulsome. This began to change as the 20th century dawned. For one, Tex's health was increasingly compromised. He had transferred many daily responsibilities to his son John, all the while aware of the need to retain his profile and input with the team. The next generation of Simones maintained this business-like approach to the team's function and its continuing presence in Syracuse. Attendance, in fact, far surpassed the numbers attained during many of Tex's best seasons.

Two other factors were now at work. The Chiefs' community-ownership model was providing less security for the future. Shares sold to supporters in the franchise's early years were often lost, forgotten, or simply not valued by later generations who might have assumed them on the death of their original benefactor. It became increasingly difficult to count on a "50 percent plus one" shareholder attendance or set of proxies to vote on team business at the annual meeting. Tex was one of the first to recognize this challenge. In a way, the team's under-financing had always been an issue. In their inaugural days, so eager were the Los Angeles Dodgers to divest themselves of the one-time Montreal Royals franchise that Dodgers' ownership representative Buzzie Bavasi had even foregone the original request of $50,000 for an eventual asking price of $35,000, an amount Syracuse citizens had still been unable raise through the sale of community shares. The shortfall was forgiven by the Dodgers.

There is nothing intrinsically wrong about such a community-ownership model as the Green Bay Packers of the National Football League prove to this day. It cannot be solely a one-time, quickly forgotten charitable donation. Shareholders needed to pay at least some attention to the business requirements of an annual meeting and the obligations attendant upon a financial shortfall. As well, the organization requires a steady and reliable income source, such as NFL teams enjoy from their lucrative television deals. Tex partially resolved these issues by ensuring the team either broke even, made a small profit, or, in one case, relied on the generosity of the Toronto Blue Jays. And with the annual payback of the loan to build the stadium of over $750,000 a year, Tex sacrificed short-term gain for long-term stability. As for the matter of a "50 percent plus one" annual meeting participation, he worked through the Board to reduce the obligation for attendance by shareholders, or their proxy representative, to 33% of the share total. But the Board, to whom he reported, was increasingly made up of a new generation of community leaders as well as investors for whom business concerns weighed as heavily on their minds as the community stewardship role. Without disparaging their emphasis and assuming they had the city's interest at heart their role was nevertheless now more intrusive into the team's day-to-day operation. The team President hired new staff members who took over the sales end of the team and regulated John to the operation of baseball related duties. The financial responsibilities were taken out of his control, and private meetings behind closed doors began with both Tex and John being left out.

As well, new Board members were prepared to buy more shares even though the team bylaws limited their voting power. This also would change as the franchise experienced financial setbacks which its broad-based community share model was unable to sustain, particularly since so many of the original small shareholders or their heirs regarded their "investment" as a charitable donation rather than a business obligation. By 2013, the Board welcomed bidders who would contribute financially to relieve the team's debt burden, brought on by ballpark upgrades, ongoing issues with the county over its annual rental fee, attendance uncertainty, and the amounts potentially owed to Tex and John Simone as their retirement annuities. In so doing, investors were promised additional equity in the team.

Sensing a change was in the works, John enlisted the support of an old friend who was interested in owning a minor league baseball team. He quickly put together a group of investors with net worth in the billions of dollars that included the President of Jetblue, David Barger, and Canadian Businessman Bill Yuill. John Simone and his partner, Toronto businessman and former Blue Jay employee Elliott Wahle, actually bid more, but the Board went with a lower amount from the rival group, ostensibly because they felt the latter provided a more secure guarantee for the team remaining in Syracuse under local ownership. It was a guarantee which, while it could be stated, could never be absolutely ensured. If losses continued and there was no foreseeable likelihood of new money from local investors, it would almost certainly mean the team would either have to leave town or find out-of-town investors with their own agendas.

The decision of the Chiefs' Board to go with a new set of financiers ensured that the Simone family's 53-year relationship with the Syracuse Chiefs would almost certainly end. John Simone recalled the process that followed. "My decision to not be part of the new administrative structure was inevitable, though it took almost two weeks for the new ownership group to actually take over. I was told to fire my entire staff, something I was not going to do. The new administration needed to figure out how to get control of the office without violating the labor laws and remaining in good standing with the International League, which was not very happy with the situation. The International League President, Randy Mobley, asked the new group and me to discuss the situation going forward. In the Chiefs' Board Room, Mobley asked the organization to keep me on in some capacity to ensure that league matters wouldn't be compromised.

Chiefs management agreed with Mobley and the wishes of the league. I had decided that I would not be the one employee who would survive.

"I appreciated Randy and the league intervening on my behalf, but I had no interest in working with this group, so I declined. Mobley then asked if I would stay on until a suitable replacement was hired. As a favor to the league that had been so good to me over the years, I agreed. It took another three weeks for my replacement to arrive. With my office packed up and ready to vacate, the team's lawyer let me know the team's treasurer would be informing the remaining employees they would be terminated that day. At 5:00 pm on October 6, 2013, I walked out of that stadium for the final time."

It may have been John's last day, but not Tex's. A few months before the Board had named him Vice-President Emeritus, an apparently nice way of relieving him of the title of Vice-President and Chief Operating Officer. As you can imagine, Tex was not pleased, but it was a signal the end was near. "Acting as my father's agent," John recalled, "I informed the Board that my dad would go ahead with the change in titles and agree to retire without pay if his annuity could be exercised and put in force."

The team's assets included annuities owned by the team payable to Tex and John or half of the team's cash. The team agreed to sign off on the transaction, something for which there was no guarantee in the future. These payments, together with a new video board, financial losses from the previous season, and legal fees to engineer the change in ownership, put the team in a precarious position requiring further investment. The new group could run through the team's cash flow, blame the losses on Tex to gain control and acquire the team's treasury stock in exchange for cash to keep the team afloat. It was a plan a few years in the making and, in the end, was almost foiled by the group John put together so fast.

Once a new staff had assembled, the team's Board leadership was surprised by the appearance of Tex Simone. After all, the new role allowed Tex to keep his office even though he was now an advisor. The team's new General Manager was told to ask Tex to vacate his office, but he was reluctant. Tex stayed until December 21st. His health was declining, and so the family contacted the new management team. As John recalls, "We told them we would like to move my dad out of his office. We arranged for it to happen at night when everyone was gone. We told Tex what was happening, and surprisingly, he agreed to leave. So, at 9:00 pm on December 21st, we backed up our vehicles to the front of the stadium and began to box up over 50 years of history as we vacated the stadium. Tex was there and stayed awhile before giving up and leaving us to finish. It was emotional for him, I'm sure, but he accepted it and never looked back."

TEX'S LAST YEARS

Walking away from the team after the upheaval in team management and ownership, as well as his various illnesses and advancing Alzheimer's disease, robbed Tex of the pleasure he might have taken in the team's fortunes over his last years. "The departure from the Chiefs was a messy one," the *Post-Standard* reported, "Having been pushed out of his position in the fall of '13 by a new board of directors in search of a fresh vision, he remained on the scene as a ceremonial adviser to the club. But his health and his pride wouldn't allow him to continue for long in that role … and in December, Tex, frail and sad, walked away with a sigh." The new group promised a "Tex Simone Day" the next season, but that never happened, and Tex missed his only chance at it during his final season in 2014. It would take the owner of the Syracuse Crunch Hockey team Howard Dolgon to recognize Tex before a playoff game at the Onondaga County War Memorial for his achievements in baseball and to the community.

He died on March 6, 2015. The accolades were fulsome, genuine, and touching, though no one seemed ready to discuss the events of the past two years and the freezing out of his family. Pat Gillick called him a true, true baseball man, former Chiefs president Don Waful described him as the organization's guiding light; Elliott Wahle said, "He touched a lot of people with a lot of decency that's hard to come by." Hall of Fame field manager Bobby Cox, who played and managed in Syracuse, said, "He cared about the players. He was one of us." Other accolades described him as a savior of the franchise and as a veritable Houdini for his ability to get the franchise out of any sticky situations they faced.

Tex's honors were many. They included multiple halls of fame, including the Greater Syracuse Sports Hall of Fame in 1991, the Syracuse Chiefs Wall of Fame (2001), the International League Hall of Fame (2008), Le Moyne College Hall of Fame (2011), and the North High School Hall of Fame (2012). There was civic recognition by the city of Syracuse including the Mayor's Achievement Award in 1979, the Chamber of Commerce Community Citizen Award in 1985, and the Joseph Pietrafesa Memorial Award for outstanding citizenship in 1990. He won five Minor League Executive of the Year awards, one of which he shared with son John in 1998. He was awarded the President's Trophy from Minor League Baseball in 1987.

The *Syracuse Post-Standard* summed up Tex Anthony Simone's legacy.

When it comes to Anthony "Tex" Simone, it was more a matter of keeping baseball in our town than just the business of baseball itself.

"… if it had not been for Tex Simone's efforts in the early 1990s, the team would not be at that existing ballpark (now NBT Bank Stadium)," International League President Randy Mobley said, "And may not be in that city for that matter."

Savior of the franchise … Patriarch of modern-day baseball in Syracuse.

Yes, indeed. Job well done!

Personal messages were noted as follows:

He was predeceased by his six siblings, Archie Simone, Marie DeGroot, Ann Santola, Nicholas "Nick" Simone, Louise Michaels, and Dominic Simone.

*Tex is **survived** by his loving wife of 59 years, Joanne (Venditti) Simone; his two children, Wendy (Steven) Shoen of Syracuse and John (Mary) Simone of North Syracuse; six grandchildren, Andrew, Adam, Ariel, Alexander, Aaron, and Karen; many nieces, nephews, and cousins.*

His family wishes to express special thanks to Becca Quilty-Koval and the 2nd-floor staff at St. Joseph's Hospital, Joanne Kolo, and the entire staff at the VA Medical Center, 5th Floor, 7th Floor, and emergency room doctors and nurses. Jenna Gardner at Upstate ENT. Sue Edwards for her compassionate care, and Bob Snyder for his assistance with this obituary.

*A **Funeral Mass** in celebration of Tex Simone's life will be conducted at 10 am on Tuesday, March 10, 2015, at Our Lady of Pompei/St. Peter Church. Entombment will follow in Woodlawn Cemetery Mausoleum.*

POSTSCRIPT

The new managers of the baseball team's fortunes were as subject to the same business challenges the previous community-ownership model had faced. They had one benefit, however, the increasing value of Minor League Franchises in general. As such, they were well positioned for a healthy return on their initial 2013 investment. The team was eventually sold for a handsome profit to the New York Mets baseball organization. The team passed from local ownership to one controlled by a major league team. The Mets promised to maintain their immediate presence in Syracuse but could give no long-term assurances. Remaining in Syracuse would rely on business considerations, not sentiment, the latter being the priceless commodity Tex traded in because he believed in it for so many years.

The one-time debate about the team's name offending Indigenous people and for which Tex had seemingly reached a reasonable compromise in 2006 allowing for the return of the venerable Chiefs nickname was resolved by changing it to the Syracuse Mets. With it, a historic identity, regardless of its problematic character, was jettisoned, as was its continuing existence as a Syracuse-owned team. It was now part of a larger corporate entity under the control of the New York Mets.

We have no interest here in debating the merits of these developments and changes, but as they evolved over the years beyond 2013, it meant the ties were cut, and the hurt inflicted on the Simone family was best known to them. It is pointless to speculate on how Tex might have thought about all of these contemporary changes, but one thing is certain: Because of Tex Simone and his family, this ball club, its two ballparks, and the long heritage of the game among fans in Syracuse and within its surrounding communities had survived, flourished, and contributed to a ball club in another country winning two World Series, as well as providing a developmental foundation for another (Washington Nationals) winning in 2019.

Syracuse's current role as a supplier of talent for the New York Mets represented a kind of full circle for the affiliation. It went back to the Mets' first-ever spring training in St. Petersburg, Florida, in 1962 when a young Tex Simone sat next to a baseball legend, Casey Stengel, and, oh so gently, nudged him awake from a temporary slumber as the media approached. Casey is gone, as is his then-young friend from Syracuse, but the ties binding these two organizations are now on the other foot. It will be the New York Mets' oversight of the Syracuse ball club which ensures either its survival as a wide-awake presence in Syracuse's unfolding future or its end.

TEX SIMONE'S LEGACY

Tex brought imagination, commitment, and just plain hard work to overcome any possible challenges. In the difficult times for minor league baseball in the 1960s, even the most optimistic follower of the game might have questioned how long Triple-A baseball in Syracuse could overcome a nationwide negative trend for Minor League Baseball, particularly given the city's declining fortunes. Instead, a golden age for Syracuse baseball was just starting. Reasonably priced entertainment, a chance to see tomorrow's major league stars, and the city's oversized contribution to another team's World Series triumphs were just some of the guaranteed and annual blessings made possible by Tex Simone's hometown devotion.

How did he do it? For one thing, he refused to be daunted by supposedly foolproof urban equations. He would end an affiliation with baseball's greatest dynasty, the New York Yankees, when it threatened his team's independent operation. His loyalty to an expansion major league affiliate, the Toronto Blue Jays, was never easy, particularly in the early years when the talent made available to him was not of pennant-winning quality. Eventually, his loyalty to this new affiliation was a significant piece in the foundation for two World Series-winning teams. Most importantly, and ensuring the team's long-term sustainability in Syracuse, was his dogged pursuit of first an upgraded MacArthur Stadium and then, as its classic but increasingly insufficient quality became apparent, a new ballpark. His determination kept a baseball team in a city with declining population and prospects continually profitable and, therefore, stable.

You do not work for and then provide managerial oversight for an organization for over half a century without receiving a few slings and arrows from a quibbling public. An ongoing criticism was the team's limited playoff appearances during their 31 years affiliated with the Toronto Blue Jays. It is impossible to know if this record would have improved, or for that matter, been worse with another major league team. Limited playoff appearances would continue under the Washington Nationals. Under the Blue Jays affiliation, Tex was a regular part of their decision-making process. He understood, better than anyone else, the contemporary nature of such affiliations. Minor League teams are at the service of the major league team. The major league affiliate assumed the burden of player salary costs, and because of this, grateful Minor League teams have seen their value skyrocket from the days the Montreal Royals franchise was transferred to Syracuse in 1961. In those days, it was a struggle to raise even $35,000 to support its community ownership model. In 2017, the Syracuse franchise sold for $18 million. It was the long-term affiliation with Toronto that had ensured Syracuse's survival as a minor league entity from the Blue Jays' role as a guarantor of loans as well as an outright $1 million gift as a contribution to the city's new stadium.

As for the new stadium, it has occasionally been criticized as being out of the way and not central to Syracuse's downtown core. This is an odd complaint, given the ballpark's location at the same general spot since 1934. Nor does it take account of the receding importance and declining quality of Syracuse's downtown during many of those years and the benefit accruing to the team by a location on the city's northern edge. Syracuse's urban population has, for the past 50 years, been falling even as its surrounding metropolitan area was stable or expanding in places people were choosing to live. Realistically, the team's supporters needed to be drawn from this wider pool of citizens, and the ballpark was a beneficiary of this location, which, by the way, is just down the street from the Destiny USA shopping mall, a major attraction for regional residents and out of town visitors.

Another observation was the makeup of Tex's staff and the appearance of favoritism in hiring family members. This is a particularly unfair gibe given the team's precarious financial existence for much of its history. Tex implemented measures ensuring the team's economic sustainability for much of this history. It meant the team either could not pay the kinds of salaries associated with this type of work, or, if they could attract talent prepared to work for less than market value, there would be no long-term commitment. Running the team like a family operation was the necessary pre-requisite for survival, and in fact, was a model the Blue Jays, as Pat Gillick has commented, aspired to for themselves. Did such a model become increasingly problematic as the 21st century dawned? Perhaps, but the eventual sale of the team to out-of-town interests in the persons of the New York Mets baseball team, a few years after the Simones left, is all the proof one needs that another organizational model was not the answer for guaranteeing the team would always remain under local ownership. Tex's organizational structure might have had some of the mom-and-pop local store identity, but that was its saving grace. Tex managed the big stuff, including relations with the affiliate, while son John increasingly took on day-to-day management functions, and daughter Wendy oversaw merchandising and souvenirs. In the early days, Mom (Joanne) answered phones and played a general factotum role. As Wendy says, even her kids did jobs around the place, from cleaning toilets to taking tickets, all to keep the organization alive. Such dedication made baseball possible in Syracuse, New York.

One problematic area for Tex and his management team was the team's name, the Chiefs. The name might not have been an issue given its French and Latin origin long pre-dating North American colonization, but the team used a Native American image with a literal and then a stylized war bonnet as its logo. As well, it was happily referred to as the Tribe for most of its history. This issue reached a larger head during the 1995 World Series when the airwaves were dominated by the Cleveland Indians' cartoonish Chief Wahoo caricature and the tomahawk chop of the Atlanta Braves fans. Tex sought an accommodation with the local Onondaga leadership, but Chief Irving Powless said nothing would assuage their concerns. The team's name and its identifying images had to go. By the next year, the team was known as the SkyChiefs in honor of central New York's rich aviation history. In 2006, after Tex's discussions with the local tribe members, he was able to reach an accommodation, and Syracuse returned to the Chiefs' name. Elsewhere, Cleveland phased out Chief Wahoo, and for the 2022 season, the team was renamed the Guardians.

Over the years, there were occasional complaints that the team's budget was not overseen rigorously (or, to use later language descriptions of this process – micro-managed) by the Board, to which Tex reported. Tex's ability to generate a modest profit every year had earned him the respect of his Board. Never was there anything scandalous or inappropriate about his management of the Chiefs. Nor did anyone quibble about his son John taking over the GM reins. He had learned from the best in the business. The Board under which Tex worked for years was beyond grateful for the manner in which he not only trained his successor, but then remained on the scene to mentor and support him. Few organizations are so gifted. And like his dad, John turned down many offers to move on to other more lucrative positions, including from the Blue Jays organization.

AN ABIDING FAITH

lzheimer's took a toll in Tex's later years, but nothing interfered with his deep and abiding faith. A habit of driving in the wrong direction on a one-way street despite protestations from family members eventually brought a need for them to chauffeur him. It became a daily pattern. On Saturday morning, for instance, it was mass at the Dominican (Nuns) Monastery, where he was the only person known to be allowed to go behind the counter to pray with the nuns. On other days, it might be a journey to the Assumption Church Food Pantry to donate food or money, depending on the needs at the time. His regular place of worship at 7:00 am every Monday through Friday was Our Lady of Pompeii Church, where he and Joanna had been married so many years before. Tex donated a piece of art to the church, and it was here on Sunday mornings he had ushered at the 8:00 am mass.

Regardless of what family member brought him, they'd all have to park in the same spot, or he wouldn't get out. Then he'd look up to the top of the church roof and point to the cross. He might be greeted at the door by Sister Elizabeth (though well into her nineties, she continued visiting nursing homes, hospitals, and the housebound to bring the Eucharist). Once inside, Tex sat in the same pew every day. Around 7:20, he'd rise and stop at the various statues, including St. Anthony and St Michael. He'd light a candle for someone, stop in the center of the church at the crucifix, and then finish at the Blessed Mother. It was a routine he never abandoned.

Family

Ultimately, the Tex Simone story is about family. For Tex's oldest child daughter, Wendy Shoen, it begins with her own memories.

"My dad was just a small-town guy at heart, but he had such a big presence about him. When I went to the Baseball Winter Meetings in the later years, and even after I was no longer working in the sport, there was never a time that someone wouldn't stop me and ask about my dad. After his passing, so many people stopped to tell me how they missed seeing my dad at the meetings. He had that way about him. He touched people's hearts, even if it was just in a brief meeting. His love for people, and especially kids, was who he was.

"His annual trip with players to the children's hospital in Syracuse was probably one of his favorite things. In the last few years of our time with the Chiefs, I was doing all the Community Relations visits with the players. The last year we went to the hospital in 2013, I had set up the visit. When I reminded Dad it was time to go, his Alzheimer's had apparently robbed him of any memory of the commitment. My daughter and I tried to get him to remember, but ultimately, we failed and had to leave without him. It would be the first year he would not attend.

"I cried because I knew how much it meant to him every year. When we arrived at the hospital with the players, we proceeded as normal, but all the nurses, of course, asked where my dad was. I said he wasn't feeling good as I didn't want them to know he couldn't remember. After about 10 minutes into the visit with the kids, I turned around and guess who had arrived? My dad! He had remembered, and when he got there he cried either from the happiness of actually remembering or out of sadness from possibly missing it. It was a beautiful and heart-warming visit, as always. As he had done in previous years, he hugged the little children with a big smile on his face. After the visit, as was his practice, he took all the players out to lunch to thank them. It will always be one of my fondest memories."

Tex influenced Wendy's children in so many essential ways.

For Andrew Shoen, a personal trainer, it was his grandfather's belief in the American dream. "He worked his way from the bottom to the top, but he never felt better than anyone. If necessary, he'd join the stadium sweepers or the grounds crew and, on occasion, even throw batting practice. I try to follow his work ethic of getting up every morning with the attitude he instilled in me of let's get going and get done what needs to be taken care of."

Adam Shoen recalls, "His life story influenced mine. I grew up at the stadium and have pretty much spent most of my time there throughout my whole life, including up until now as I work for the food and beverage company currently at the stadium. I liked being there from a young age, so I think it kind of keeps me wanting to still work there today."

For Ariel Shoen, who now works for high-profile ballplayers and their families, meeting their off-field personal needs, "I learned so much from him, particularly the way he carried himself when he faced the adversity of memory loss and physical decline. He was a proud man and had been so lively and charismatic. Now, he had to find ways to cope. He'd keep notes telling him what to do. He did a good job of concealing it from us, but in the end, we had to learn to love a different, almost new, person."

For John Simone's children, there are these special memories. "Alexander John Simone was born on March 26, 1992, and Grandpa Tex was the first person father John saw when he came out of the maternity room. Tex had a great smile on his face when told it was a boy. He loved holding him as a baby. As a child, Alex got to hang around the ballpark, just like his dad did, and would often be playing catch with Carlos Delgado, Robert Perez, Ray Giannelli, Howard Battle, and others on the field as a youngster. Later, he was thrown into the dugout at seven years old and handled the duties as a batboy before then working in the clubhouse washing clothes and cleaning cleats. At 15 years old, when Tex lost his license because of a car crash, he asked Alex to drive him to church. Alex had to explain to him that he couldn't because he didn't have his driver's license yet. Alex had the most interaction with him because of the time he spent at the ballpark. He loved his grandfather very much."

Aaron Anthony Simone was born on July 24, 1997. It was the first year of the new stadium – and it happened to be Bat Night. At eight years old, he also followed his brother on the field as a batboy and loved being out there. He would often drive around with Tex on the stadium golf cart, picking up home run balls during batting practice.

Karen Grace Simone was born on August 27, 1999. Tex loved her curly hair as a baby. While she didn't spend much time at the ballpark, she loved seeing her grandpa whenever she came to the park.

Uncle Elliott

There was an important family relation without whom Tex's many talents may never have fully blossomed. Tex spent his years from the age of 13 until his service years at 625 Darlington Road, a house owned by his sister's husband, Elliott DeGroot, who worked as an engineer with Lamson Engineering Company. John Simone recalls, "He had purchased the two-story family house and occupied the bottom flat with my Aunt Marie, while my grandparents lived on the second floor with the remaining children in the household – Tex and his brothers Archie and Dominick. They would often house boarders from Italy who came over looking for work, including my grandmother's brother, Uncle Dan, who paid rent and helped the family buy food."

"My Uncle Elliott was a sports guy," John says. "He recognized that Tex was the most gifted athlete in the family and had the discipline to get better, that his talented younger brother Dom lacked. Elliott made sure that my dad had sneakers and baseball equipment. He tricked my grandfather into thinking Tex had a job by giving him money for the pretend job that he didn't have so that he could keep playing basketball, football, and baseball. Tex even spent an extra year in high school to continue to play sports. Elliott would often meet my father in Jersey City, Atlanta, or Toronto if he was there on business and buy him dinner after a road game and hang out with the players. He was also the person who paid for my dad's trip to Kissimmee, Florida, to enroll in the Gus Mauch's Training School."

"When my dad was a trainer in the 1960s, my uncle Elliott's son Richard worked in the clubhouse picking up and washing uniforms. As GM in the 1990s, my dad hired Uncle Elliott's grandsons, Elliott and Garrett, to run the visiting clubhouse at old MacArthur Stadium while they were in college. Garrett later became a trainer in the Toronto Blue Jays organization, working in Medicine Hat, Kinston, and Knoxville before leaving to work at the University of Central Florida. As you could guess, Tex had asked the Blue Jays to hire him out of college. Elliott played baseball at Johns Hopkins University and then later joined the FBI before working for the National Security Agency. In between his Government work with both agencies, he continued to play baseball in a 30-plus age league. My father would always make sure to send him bats, gloves, or any equipment he needed; I'm sure remembering what his grandfather had done for him."

A RECOMMENDATION
BY WILLIAM HUMBER

I was fortunate, between 1979 and 2011, to lead 25-weekend trips for baseball supporters to Syracuse for a ballgame, and then afterward, we went on to Cooperstown for its Hall of Fame main street pleasures. We did this twenty consecutive times through 1998, and then between 2003 and 2011, I led the final five visits, usually in the off years. While the Hall of Fame visit to Cooperstown might have been each trip's selling point, the personal high points for everyone were our regular meetings with Anthony Tex Simone, General Manager and later Senior Vice-President for the Syracuse Chiefs International League team.

Over the years, despite his dealings with notable baseball personalities, no one was more generous, affable, and genuinely pleased to see us than Tex Simone. Of course, Syracuse was the Toronto Blue Jays' Triple-A affiliate. Another person might have felt he'd fulfilled his obligation to the major league city by meeting us at least the first time for a brief afternoon overview, then thanked us for coming and hoped we enjoyed the night's ballgame. But he did this every year, always aware there might be someone on this year's trip who had not heard the Chiefs' story before. He would let us roam the field afterward. I well remember my seven-year-old son throwing off the pitcher's mound on one occasion, and, many years later, and now a much older college student, he assumed the stadium announcer's role for several innings.

I had first contacted the Syracuse Chiefs in the early spring of 1979, the year after they had become the Blue Jays Triple-A affiliate. Clarence Fineberg, a man who lived in my parent's condominium in Florida, had suggested I write to Tex. Clarence had once sold concessions at Syracuse's MacArthur Stadium and told me Tex would be happy to hear from me. The Chiefs had abandoned the mighty Yankees for the development challenges of an expansion baseball team, which was Canada's second major league entry. I told Tex I was planning to bring down a group who had just completed the first offering of my continuing education class at Seneca College in Toronto, appropriately named Baseball Spring Training for Fans. The premise of this Saturday morning, January through early March, course was to provide fans with, as best as possible, a classroom equivalent to what players would be doing in Florida, namely preparing for the season ahead.

The difference was that ours was a kind of hot stove conversation excuse to talk baseball in the winter months. No one in my classes ever ran laps or did push-ups, though one year, we did venture to the one-time site of old Maple Leaf Stadium at the foot of Bathurst Street and played a makeshift game on the now-sodded lawn. Soon after, the site was redeveloped as an extensive condo development, and we have ever since claimed to have played the last game where the International League Leafs toiled between 1926 and 1967, which Tex visited on multiple occasions. In 2024, the class celebrated its 46th year on the ever-popular Zoom platform.

The kindness shown to our group of traveling fans by Tex became an annual treat. It might be helping someone get the autograph of an obscure ballplayer because one of our travelers had picked up that player's sold-off jersey in another city. It might be because someone just wanted to meet a favorite player. On one occasion, Tex brought over Kelly Gruber to greet a young fan, but poor Kelly thought he was getting a call-up to the Jays. He was not, but he was very gracious. Sometimes, it was just an opportunity to get one's picture taken with the team's mascot, Scooch.

Often, Tex would dip into what remained from some recent give-away evening, like a hat or pennant, and made sure each of us received one. We always got the discounted group rate, and it never seemed we paid enough for all the courtesies he extended. On the other hand, we would take care of any shortfall at that night's game with significant purchases of Saranac beer, MacArthur's legendary Italian sausages, and the equally decadent salted potatoes. He also brought his son John, at first his assistant GM and then later the fully-fledged GM, into these conversations. It began a long-time friendship culminating in this book also involving John's sister Wendy, who, behind the scenes, quietly handled the team's merchandising.

I vividly recall our last visit to Syracuse in 2011. We were on our way to Cooperstown for the induction of Pat Gillick and Roberto Alomar into the National Baseball Hall of Fame. By then, the Chiefs had switched affiliations to the Washington Nationals. As a result, we did not make a big thing of our visit. We also knew Tex had not been well, so while hoping to see him in Syracuse, we were respectful of what might be his necessary absence. But he was at the game and was thrilled to see us. It was a particularly hot evening, and Tex favored us with one last series of gifts – his presence, his happiness at being with us, and ice cream bars for the entire group. Tex lived a full life and died in 2015, but his legacy continues in his family and in an International League team that defied the odds by remaining in the same city.

In writing this story, something stands out: the absence in the National Baseball Hall of Fame in Cooperstown of plaques recognizing the tireless, long-term, and committed work of Minor League executives. They have kept baseball alive and flourishing far from the major leagues. They have mentored and supported the climb to the top rung of baseball play for the game's next generation of superstars and regular performers, managers, and future leaders. They have been the glue holding together the edifice of organized baseball. Their future is uncertain following the impact of the pandemic beginning in 2020 and Major League Baseball's increasing control over its developmental colleagues. The Syracuse Chiefs, as a community-owned entity, and even their last name, are no more having been replaced by the New York Mets and their identifying moniker.

So here is a simple proposal. Every few years, regardless of the future form the minor leagues take, a special committee of the Hall of Fame should consider an executive from the ranks of this essential component of organized baseball for admission to the Hall.

The first choice would be easy ... Syracuse's Anthony "Tex" Simone.

FUNNY THING HAPPENED ON THE WAY TO THE BALLPARK

North High 40 CBA 27

While playing basketball at North High, his team defeated the vaunted Christian Brothers Academy in 1947 when Tex scored 27 of the 40 points to out-duel the team's best player, Regis King. Some years later, when his son attended CBA, he would often be found looking into the school's trophy case, knowing that his achievements that night stopped an undefeated season.

Angel Scull

During his days as a trainer, one of his duties would be to also take care of the clubhouse for the players and provide them with soap, towels, and other things. One year, he was spending a great deal of money on aftershave. He later found out that the teams' outfielder, Angel Scull from Cuba, enjoyed the taste of Acqua Velva, which, interestingly enough, was made with vodka, gin, lemon-lime, and blue curacao.

Bill Faul

The Ohio native was defined as a free spirit who, in 1964, went 11-1 for the Chiefs and credited Tex for helping him to hypnotize himself in the mirror before he would go out and pitch.

Willie Horton

The Detroit Tigers Hall of Fame outfielder was only 20 years old when Tex met him, and a common practice for baseball players in the 1960s was to ask the trainer for a "greenie" before the game started. Greenies were amphetamines that helped players play every day. Tex was careful with who he gave them to and thought that the 20-year-old Horton was not ready for them. So, he would buy M&M's, take out all the green ones, and give them to Horton when he requested one.

Ray Oyler

Tex would always say he was the best shortstop he ever saw, and the two were very close. With Tex, one night after a game in Buffalo, he felt pain in his stomach and was rushed to the emergency room for stomach ulcer surgery. Ray made Tex hold his hand until he went under.

John Sullivan, Jackie Moore, Gene Lamont, and Jim Leyland

All four were catchers in the Tigers organization when Tex was there, and all became managers, coaches, and one Hall of Famer. Late in Tex's career, Jim Leyland saw Tex in Spring Training when the Tigers played the Nationals and ducked out of a press conference to talk to his former Trainer. The two told stories of their tiger days, and the media waited until they were done.

The Maternity Ward

Often, players would be on the road when their wives were ready to give birth, and on occasion, Tex would get a call to get their husbands back to Syracuse. Sometimes, they didn't make it back in time, and Tex would be the surrogate father. It happened with Blue Jays first baseman Willie Upshaw's wife, Cindy, who gave birth to their first child, Clay. Later, his manager Doug Ault's wife Julie would ask for Tex to help out for the birth of their son Joshua.

Players Wives

They all adored Tex, and many credit him for saving careers like Bonnie Guidry for her husband, Ron. His favorite wife of all time had to be Shelly Pederson, whose husband, Stu, spent parts of five seasons here. He would tell Toronto to resign Stu each year just to take care of Shelly and the kids.

George Bell

The 1987 American League MVP would spend his early years in Syracuse. After getting hit by a pitch in the face that required surgery to wire his jaw, Pat Gillick called Tex to tell him that since he would not be able to play for the remainder of the season, he was going to have both his knees operated on as well. So, later that day, George woke up and couldn't eat or walk. Tex would bring his wife to the grocery store each day until he was able to travel back to Florida.

International League Meetings

As the Chairman of the International League Finance Committee and later serving as Vice President of the league, Tex was very vocal at meetings. One of his favorite decrees that, to this day, is still in the league's bylaws when voting on an amendment when asked how long Tex replied, "until the end of time."

Danny Ainge

Danny Ainge played in Syracuse after one year at BYU and was only 18 years old. The only person close to his age in the clubhouse was Tex's son, John, who would bring him to various city parks to play pick-up basketball. The two never lost a game.

Tony Fernandez

Nineteen-year-old Octavio Tony Fernandez made his debut in AAA during the final month of the season with the Chiefs. Tex got the call from Pat Gillick that the teen sensation would be joining the club and promised to take care of the youngster from the Dominican Republic.

The Simone family made sure Tony had everything he needed to live on his own in a foreign country, including curtains, a sofa, and a television. As an extra bit of care and concern, Tex would often give him a ride home after the game.

Choo-Choo Coleman

Choo-Choo Coleman, a catcher in the New York Mets organization in 1962, was called up to the Mets that season after batting only .195 with the Chiefs. He told Tex that he would be back in a few days and wouldn't make arrangements for my wife to travel to New York with me. A month later his wife went back to their hometown in Florida and Coleman finished the season with the Mets and became a fan favorite. Casey Stengel once complimented his speed, saying he'd never seen a catcher so fast at retrieving passed balls.

Ed Kranepool

Ed Kranepool was only 17 years old when he was signed by the Mets out of High School in 1962, and the first person to greet him in a professional baseball clubhouse was Tex. A team loaded with veterans, Tex took care of the youngster until he was sent to Auburn to finish the season.

Phil Regan

Phil Regan was a veteran major league pitcher who spent a few months in Syracuse during the 1964 season. Tex helped him recover from arm trouble that season and he would end up pitching in the 1966 World Series with the Dodgers the next season.

Leo Marentette

Leo Marenette was a prankster and once appeared on the local late-night Monster Movie Show that was hosted by the team's public address announcer, Mike Price. Price was a friend of Tex's and starred as the vampire character named Baron Damone. Marentette surprised Price and dressed up as a vampire one night after a game and appeared on the show.

Cecil Perkins

Cecil Perkins was a hard-throwing pitcher in the Yankees organization and played in Syracuse in 1967. During one of his outings, a hard grounder was hit back at him and caught him in the throat. He picked up the ball and got the runner out but then collapsed to the ground, unable to catch his breath. Tex ran out to provide his help and ultimately helped Perkins to breathe again.

David Wells

David Wells won over 200 games as a major league pitcher and made over 60 million dollars during his career. But before all that, he played in Syracuse and made $1,500 a month. That wasn't enough to keep him hydrated on weekends, and he often stopped in Tex's office to borrow a few dollars to get through until the next payday. Tex always had $50 for the lefthander. Later during his career when Wells saw him, he would ask Tex if he needed to borrow $50.

Todd Stottlemyre

Todd Stottlemyre was the son of Yankees great Mel Stottlemyre and spent parts of three seasons in Syracuse 1987-89. Tex had previously spent time with Mel when he was the trainer for the Yankees in 1967 and '68. When Todd arrived, Tex made sure he had everything he needed and would often pick up Todd's mom at the airport when she came in to see her son pitch.

Fred Stanley

Fred Stanely was a light-hitting infielder who came over to the Yankees organization in 1973 and helped perfect the loading of a bat with cork. Fred enlisted one of the groundskeepers to drill a cylinder hole about six inches deep in one of his bats one day. He then stuffed cork from wine bottles inside and would later top it off with a wooden cup. Fred hit two home runs that season and had the most extra-base hits in any season of his career. After his time in Syracuse, he played several years with the Yankees, and coincidently, his roommate Craig Nettles was suspended for ten games when his bat was found to have ten superballs spill out during a game in Chicago.

Bob Polinsky

Bob Polinsky was a young pitcher from Pennsylvania who joined the team in 1976. That season, he met a young lady named Karen Szombathy, interestingly enough, the daughter of Joe Szombathy, a Syracuse University football coach back when Tex was the trainer there. The two ended up getting married, and Tex was invited to the wedding. He was later traded to the White Sox for a shortstop named Bucky Dent.

Larry Murray

Larry Murray had played only nine games with the Chiefs in 1977 when Tex received a call from Gabe Paul, the Yankees General Manager, to tell him he was traded to Oakland. When Tex told him the game had started and Murray was in center field during the first inning, Paul told him to go get him before he got hurt. So, Tex went down on the field and instructed his manager to take Murray out of the game because he was traded just minutes ago.

Dennis Werth

Dennis Werth played in Syracuse in 1977 and briefly in the major leagues with the Yankees and Royals. While in Syracuse, he would ask Tex for the cracked bats that had accumulated over the season. During the off-season, Werth would make lamps out of them. Of course, Tex received one, and Dennis would go on to continue the hobby after his career ended. Twenty-five years later, his son Jayson Werth would join the Chiefs and stopped in to confirm to his dad that Tex still had the lamp in his office.

Ron Shepherd

Ron Shepherd was a top prospect for the Blue Jays, and in 1983, he decided to get married at home plate in between games of a double-header. Tex gave away the bride Janda at home plate, and the players were all in attendance in front of a packed crowd. Ron would later become a Reverend in Kilgore, Texas, his hometown.

Tom Henke

Tom Henke joined the Chiefs in 1985 and was the most dominant pitcher in team history until his eventual call-up to the Blue Jays in August. Henke was a mason during the off-season and lived across the street from Tex in the Rugby Apartments at that time. During that summer, Henke would spend the mornings digging up Tex's patio and fixing the concrete.

Cecil Fielder & Kash Beauchamp

Cecil and Kash spent part of the 1986 season with the Chiefs and were best friends as they came up through the Blue Jays system. Kash's dad, Jim, managed the Chiefs from 1981-84 and became good friends with Tex. He asked Tex to take care of his son when he joined the Chiefs. Tex was able to rent a house in the area he grew up in for Kash and his buddy Cecil, who also brought along with him his son Prince.

Bob Wishnevski, Bob Bailor, and Lindsay Kramer

Bob Bailor managed the team from 1988-91 and was one of Tex's favorite managers. During the 1989 season, Bob decided to have fun with a young reporter who he thought asked annoying questions. Short on pitching for a series vs the Toledo Mud Hens, the Blue Jays sent young right-handed pitcher Rob Wishnevski to make a spot start. Rob pitched great, and after the game, Kramer asked Bailor about his performance.

At that moment, Bailor suggested that he did well despite the fact he is really left-handed and decided to pitch right-handed today. Kramer bit and went out to question the youngster's odd ability.

Wishnevski, a rookie, went along with the ruse and was now part of the joke. Kramer and the Syracuse Post Standard printed the story despite the absurdity of it.

The next day, the Editor of the paper, who read in disbelief, asked Tex how true it was. Tex informed him that his manager told the reporter a story, never thinking it would make it past the editors. Well, it did, and they now wanted Toronto to fire Bailor immediately. After Blue Jays brass Pat Gillick and Gord Ash stopped laughing, Tex asked Bob to apologize to the reporter and the paper.

Ed Sprague

Ed Sprague spent parts of four years in Syracuse and was the only player/mascot to get thrown out of a game twice. Late in a game, Sprague argued a called third strike and was tossed by the home plate umpire. The game then went 18 innings, and during the 17th, with only die-hard fans still in attendance, out came the team's mascot Scooch, who had long retired for the evening. Only this time it was Sprague who was in the costume, and he was making a beeline for the home plate umpire. A few minutes later, the umpire tossed Sprague. The next day, the league sent a fine for his actions, which Tex took care of for the entertainment he provided on a late night.

Ryan Thompson

Ryan Thompson was an outfielder on the 1992 team and was traded to the New York Mets mid-season for David Cone. Toronto told Tex to get Ryan to New York as soon as possible because he would be joining the Mets. When Thompson showed up to the stadium to pick up his equipment, he had two plastic bags full of his clothes. Tex knew he couldn't send him to New York like that and brought him to a local luggage store and bought him two suitcases.

Ray Giannelli

Ray Giannelli was an infielder from Brooklyn. Ray's dad played for the team back in the 1956 season and the fact that he was Italian made him one of Tex's favorites. Geno's parents would visit often, and Tex would make sure they were taken care of and would take them to area Italian restaurants to eat.

Memories

Pat Gillick on Tex Simone (Hall of Fame executive Pat Gillick oversaw and was part of World Series-winning teams in Toronto and Philadelphia).

I really got to know Tex Simone when I came to the Toronto Blue Jays along with Elliott Wahle as Toronto was preparing for their first season in the American League in 1977. The Blue Jays and Syracuse Chiefs became partners through an affiliation the next year and it was apparent to me our relationship would not only be business-like but also one of extraordinary friendship. Tex, his wife Joanne, and children Wendy and John were a family operation. It was an approach we eventually hoped to build in Toronto, both very professional but also highly personal.

Looking back, I had gone to the New York Yankees from Houston in 1974, working in player development and scouting. At the time, Bobby Cox was managing the Syracuse Chiefs under General Manager Tex Simone. The Chiefs were the Yankees' number one farm team. In 1976, Bobby managed them to the Governor's Cup title. A year later, he joined the Yankees as a coach under Billy Martin.

Elliott Wahle and I first met Tex at this time. It soon became apparent to us that all he wanted was what was best for his city. It was in his heart. However, I always felt the organizational relationship had essentially been a one-way street with the Yankees. Come hell or high water, they'd always prevail. The relationship we had developed with Tex might have played a role in Syracuse eventually leaving the Yankees the next year and going with us even though the Yankees had been in the World Series.

Decisions affecting Toronto and Syracuse were, as best possible, mutually agreed upon. Tex knew the role of a minor league affiliate was to develop players for the major league team. He could make his point of view known, but at the end of the day, he understood and supported the decisions we had to make. I can't ever remember us having a major disagreement or dispute.

At the same time, he reported to a Board of Directors and wanted to put the best product on the field, so going with an expansion team was a challenge.

We did everything we could to help him. He was like your next-door neighbor, one with whom you have a mutual trust and is someone you can count on. His word was his bond. He had a warm style and engaging personality, but he knew what he wanted. His major push was getting a new stadium. It was important for business purposes but also for making the ballpark a place people wanted to be. And he succeeded. I miss him a lot. I respected him. The Blue Jays couldn't have had a better partner.

Bob Fruciano on his Friend Tex Simone (Fruciano played minor league ball in the Braves system with, amongst others, Eddie Matthews and Phil Niekro)

Tex Simone and I were lifelong friends. He was honest and caring. As a young guy, he was really quite quiet, laid back, in fact. He'd go along with what we were doing. He didn't really say much. But once he got into organized baseball with the Syracuse Chiefs, he became a real public speaker. You'd hardly know it was the same guy.

He was a really good athlete. We grew up playing sports in Schiller Park, mainly baseball and then, in the winter, in the nearby gymnasium playing basketball. In baseball, he could field and hit for power. After he got out of the military in 1954, I played softball with him on a real hot shot team, the IAAC, the Italian Amateur Athletic Club. He was our outfielder. But he really excelled in basketball. At North High School, he'd score 20 points a game at a time when teams might only score 30 in total. He brought the one-handed set shot to Syracuse. In today's game of three-point specialists, he'd be a wealthy man.

He was injured playing football, and it limited his playing time in high school. But afterward, he played on the Black and White team out of Schiller Park in Syracuse. He was a halfback, but in those days, we'd go both ways. Once, we were defensive backs and I recall intercepting a pass and making for their goal line. As I neared the sidelines, I was tackled and just had time to look around and there was Tex. I lateralled to him and he ran it the rest of the way for a touchdown.

I remember a time maybe eight or nine of us went to see a football game at Cornell. Navy was playing that day. We found a way to get into the stadium without paying, but then a security guard spotted us and started chasing Tex and me. The others got away scot-free. It wasn't looking good for us, but we ran into the Navy clubhouse and talked two guys into letting us wear their helmets, and then we ran onto the field with them. We sat the entire game on the Navy bench. You wouldn't get away with that today.

Tex got married in 1955, and I stood up for him. They had two children, Wendy and John, but they were still youngsters when Tex took quite a gamble in 1961, going to work for the new International League team that came from Montreal. He started as a groundskeeper, and there wasn't much money in that, particularly since he'd given up a good desk job as an accountant with a bakery company. But he wanted to get into baseball, and this might have been his only chance.

He moved quickly through the organization right up to General Manager by 1970. I went to almost every game, and Tex would always come and sit with me for two innings. I knew he was coming because his granddaughter, who was sitting nearby, would yell out so everyone could hear, "Here comes grandpa!"

We enjoyed the many years with the Blue Jays even though the team didn't always do well. Pat Gillick was a fantastic man. He even played in our old-timers game on two occasions. I have him on film, getting a base hit. We hated to see the Jays leave, and then they froze out Tex and John and the whole family who had taken care of everything. It all happened so quickly, and now the team is owned by the New York Mets. We've even lost our old name of the Chiefs. That hurt.

Tex was always loyal to Syracuse. He had a chance to go to Detroit with the Tigers as their trainer but I think both he and his wife didn't want to leave. He got to know all the politicians and that helped him get our new ballpark built.

He liked you if you liked him. There was no pretense to the man. He took care of everyone, even the family who might have come to their first game with a son or daughter. Tex would go back into the office and bring out a cap or ball for the child. He never held back from acknowledging your presence. He never forgot your name. He was one of those rare human beings that you can be truly thankful for knowing in your lifetime.

Gord Ash (Blue Jays General Manager and Milwaukee Brewers executive) **on Tex, John, and the Future of Baseball in Syracuse**

"Tex never thought he was bigger than anyone else. We were able to thank and help him and others in small ways. As in the case of Tom Cheek and Buck Martinez, the Jays drafted Tex's grandson, the son of John Simone.

"When John took over, there were no problems from our end. In fact, it might have been a more difficult transition for John as his father was obviously overseeing the entire operation, but I'd always talk to John first about any changes we were going to make before I talked to Tex.

"Tex was so beloved, so I was surprised when the Board went a different way in 2013. It had seemed the Simones had so many allies on the Board right up to the Chair level. Years later, we, as the Milwaukee Brewers, made some inquiries when we learned the team was for sale, but it appeared there was already a handshake, or under-the-table, agreement with the Mets before the deal was announced.

"John knew times were changing and did the best he could to adjust. Syracuse is not a big market. They'd had an old stadium for many years, and while I like Syracuse, baseball did not appear to be top of the agenda for most people. Plus, the weather is always a factor until the summer. Still, I think the franchise will continue in Syracuse with the Mets. It's a good location for them and the International is a good league to be in. The Mets themselves are going through some business changes, but Syracuse will be able to withstand any economic challenges in the future, unlike if they'd remained on their own as a community-owned team."

THE LETTERS HOME

To Archie from Your Loving Brother Tex

We are fortunate to have a series of letters, in Tex's own words, sent home to his oldest brother, Archie. They capture the occasional ordeal of Army life, its moments of freedom and discovery, and also its uncertainty as to where he might be sent, either the battlefield of Korea or the occupation forces in Europe. His abiding love of family and his hometown of Syracuse are captured in these private letters.

2 December 1950 – Things have been pretty rough for me. I went broke the second day I was in the army at Ft. Devens. I swore off craps and poker. They have some pretty big games. I have been borrowing writing paper and everything. Arch, do not mention any of these things I tell you to Ma or Pa or anybody in the family ... Every Saturday morning before inspection, we have an hour talk on the world situation by the captain and everything is laid on the line. He said this morning that everything looks pretty bad, and we get the first line dope right from Washington ... Well, Arch, as far as I know, I am in the Construction Engineers. Everyone gets six weeks of combat infantry training, which is something they didn't do the last war. After that, we will go into construction unless the world situation gets worse ... They are throwing stripes around here like they were nothing because we're the first ones in here. I am going to mind my own business and see what I can do. One kid has been in two weeks, and

he got a stripe and one for three months, and he is a corporal. **They need a lot of leaders** ... There are an awful lot of rattlers and water moccasins down here, and you have to watch your step.

Between 2 and 5 December 1950 – I see by the scores I didn't do so good. Army and Ohio State took it on the chin. Syracuse got beat, too. Well, after this week, you will be able to drop me a line because I will be at my basic training camp. I will send my address.

5 December 1950 – Archie, this is between me and you. I mean it now. If I don't come home for Christmas, I never will. We expect to be overseas by January ... right after basics. We were scheduled for France, but I don't know now. I am supposed to be in the engineers. I just got thru cleaning my carbine for inspection tomorrow, and what a job. Spic and span.

10 December 1950 – I never would have called, but I just got the itch to hear some voices from home. If I knew she [mom] was going to start to cry, I never would have called. I guess she misses me a lot. Don't worry about me gambling. I just lose two dollars and then pull out; believe me ... About Christmas, it is canceled ... We start basic training tomorrow, six weeks of it. I asked when the hell are we going to get engineer training. I got picked out of 80 men to be ahead of 17 men (platoon leader). It is a week trial and there is a rate in it.

20 December 1950 – I hope I get three days for New Year's. I'll go down to New Orleans and see the Sugar Bowl. It is about a five-hour train ride from here. I got paid today, $24 dollars ... I got a little more praise today from the C.O. (Company Commander). I was drilling the men, and he called me over. I went up to him, gave him a nice snappy salute, and he gave me an at-ease. Then he told me I was do- ing a very good job ... Today, some wise sergeant picked on me from the next barracks and gave me three days of extra duty, but that was quickly taken care of by the old man (my sergeant). So, if I can keep

my nose clean, I stand in a pretty good position. Arch, I am pretty homesick about this time, but don't tell Mom or Pop or anybody.

New Year's Eve, 31 December 1950 – I am in charge of quarters today, and there is a typewriter here in the office, so I thought I would try it out. I give all of the passes out and make sure they don't get in trouble. I also have to answer all phone calls and take all messages that come in for the officers … I like Retreat a lot. Retreat is every Friday night at 4 o'clock. It is just a salute to the colors. We dress up in a Class B uniform, which consists of your regular dress uniform with your boots and your pants bloused in your boots. You also have your helmet on, which makes it Class B. Then, you march down to the drill field. There is a band there. You stand at attention, parade past, and salute the general, and then they play the national anthem. Then, your company marches in front of the reviewing stand to pass inspection.

27 February 1951 – Next week, we take a final test, so I guess this is the last week. We're finishing up firing the machine guns this week. We fired the bazooka today. What a weapon that is. I start Construction Inspectors School on March 12th and finish on April 9th. So, when I get a furlough, I'll never know … I guess you're right about baseball being the only good sport. I signed up to try out for the camp team. They have a 154-game schedule. Art Houtteman took my application. He is in the 43rd Infantry Division, not that I mind it here … Richmond is a pretty good town. Lots of women, but you have to watch your dough. A couple of guys got rolled last week.

4 March 1951 – I got a little bad news, so don't tell Mom. I have an infected left eye, and it is all bandaged up …Tomorrow, we take the final basics test. I'm glad that it is over with, except that on Wednesday we crawl the infiltration course. Once in the day and once at night. Then, on Thursday we get the overhead artillery fire, and on Friday, we take the physical training test; then, it is really over with … I heard

that Dan Greer is home for ten days. He writes to one of the guys that is with me. He is all set to ship out to Korea. They get their shots and leave on the 17th of March. Boy, that's pretty bad news. He is with the 45th Infantry. Remember Joe Barbetta? He is on his way to Korea also … All the guys that were drafted with me and were ready for the boat to Europe, and here I still am.

5 March 1951 – My eye is healing up fast, and the bandage is off. Starting next week, ten men a week will get their furloughs. I am going to try and swing it so I make it home about the 23rd of March, so then I will catch Easter. Another reason is that maybe I'll have my stripes by then. Don't tell Mom anything. I want to surprise her. Don't tell anybody, understand? I made a little haul in the crap game on payday last week, so I am saving that to get home on. I feel kind of leery having that dough on me, though. It's not much, but it is enough.

Between 5 and 10 March 1951 – Yesterday, we went thru the infiltration course. We crawled once in the day and once in the night. Boy, that was rugged last night. It was so dark you couldn't see anything. They're firing 50 calibers over your head (three feet), and then there is TNT blowing up all around you. At night, you have to be careful not to crawl into one of their TNT holes. Of course, they're all barb-wired off, but you crawl thru barbed wire, so at night, you don't know where you are, and, boy, when you're close to those holes, it really lifts you up. Scared the s. out of me, and you keep your head down and your ass.

10 March 1951 – About me shooting craps, Arch, don't worry. I know what I am doing. I told you before I go in with a deuce and play. I just take the chance of making a hit right away so I can last in the game. If it goes, I just quit. Believe me, **I got that kind of willpower**. I am way ahead. Yesterday, I shot a little before going to Washington, and I started with a dollar. Before you knew it, I made a 32-dollar pass and

fouled up on the 50-dollar pass, but I made enough to enjoy myself on my pass. It just seems that I get that one big roll a game. When it comes me and Joe really sweep the line. I made seven naturals, two elevens, and three fives yesterday (one roll). I had a pretty good streak. I just want you to understand when I lose the two dollars we quit. That's our policy.

15 March 1951 – The first week of that school kept me pretty busy. There are only four of us privates; all the rest are sergeants bucking for Master, so you can see how important the school is. In class, they all say, ask Anthony; he probably knows. It's a 059 school ... I got a big kick out of the way Ma writes her letters. I couldn't stop laughing. Don't ever laugh at her Arch; she might stop writing. I really appreciate the letters right from her ... The weather has been awful, so we haven't been practicing baseball.

16 March 1951 – I thought I told you I started school last week. It is a pretty high-standard school. I'll be home for Easter if nothing goes wrong.

3 April 1951 – It is raining like hell out right now, and I feel sorry for them guys that are out there walking their post. It is one o'clock in the morning, and my relief is on, so that is why I am awake. Well, this is my last day of school, and I hope that I pass the final test. About moving, the rumor is that we're going to stay right here. My order for Cpl. hasn't come down yet, and I hope they pass it thru. I still don't know when I am getting my furlough. How are the Nats [Syracuse NBA team] doing? I see where they beat the Knicks at home. I went up to practice baseball on and Sun., and I don't know, I still may play. The weather has been nice and warm, and I hope that it stays that way.

6 April 1951 – **The baseball season should be opening up pretty soon and what have the Chiefs got this year?** Did they get anybody

from the Yankee chain? The Senators are playing Cinci next week in Lynchburg, about 18 miles from here. It's on a weekday but I doubt if I can sneak away... I am all thru school, and we start working Monday at the camp here. We have to enlarge the airport because they are bringing in some Air Force outfits. That's all we need here are some flyboys now. That's all you hear in this outfit is rumors. You can't believe anything until it happens. More b.s. than anything else. I made Corporal last Wednesday and I might make sergeant sooner than I thought I would. I am a non-com now, and I can go to the non-com club and go out anytime I want to that is if I don't foul up.

11 April 1951 – I was surprised when I got back. I had my corporal stripes waiting for me. I hope I make sergeant just as fast, but then that is quite a jump. I am really working, and I don't suck anybody's backside either. I just took your advice and kept my nose clean. ... I received special orders from special service to report for baseball practice every day from one to five, and it was signed by the colonel himself, so I am going to have to go. You see, it is an order now. We open against Camp Breckinridge, Kentucky, on the 26th of the month. We have 80 games to play at home and away ... I got it made pretty good here. I'd probably never be able to make a higher rate in special service ... So, the Chiefs look pretty good. Well, I hope that they do good. I was sorry to hear that the Nats lost out. I think that they could have won it.

19 April 1951 – We finished the bridge and now we are building a tank trail. It has to be strong enough to hold the new 60-ton tanks that they are going to make this summer. They will be something to look at. ... I am feeling okay, except that I am mighty homesick. I hope that I don't have to spend more than 21 months in this army. My morale is very low... The mail cheers me up ...I hope that you catch a good day for the ball game, and I wish that I was there... the capt. told me to forget about baseball because we're scheduled to move from this camp. Where we are going, I don't know. I hope that it isn't

where I think it is. They have been showing us films on Korea and the engineers for the last two weeks. I just pray that it isn't there, Arch.

25 April 1951 – I was very glad to hear that Rochester won the playoffs. Of course, I think that the Nats could have beaten them both ... The bridge came out good. I got some praise for it. About the tank trail, it is just a road leading into the firing ranges and combat courses ... We started on a dry dock pier last Monday, and it is almost done, too. It is remarkable what they do in the Army. Of course, you're always working against time so they do it the quickest and shortest way. We built a 900-yard road in a time limit for four days so that is really going. They say it takes two infantrymen to do the work of one engineer. I believe them. We are moving next week, I guess. We are going to A.P. Hill, Virginia. We will be on maneuvers for ten weeks. I am going to love that. Sleeping, eating, and showering outside for ten weeks. I hope I will last it out. I am supposed to go to leadership school, and if I make up my mind, maybe I won't have to go on maneuvers. It is a tough school. All the officers go there before going to OCS.

1 May 1951 – Friday, our Co. gets inspected by the Inspecting General, and boy, it is really chicken s..t. They test for haircuts and everything. So, now I have another G.I. haircut. The capt. gave the order. Our sergeant got a baldy, and you should see him. His head looks like a cue ball. ... So, the Chiefs are doing great. Well, I sure would like to see them go this year. We saw Washington last weekend, and they have a very good team.

11 July 1951 – *letterhead -> **Company "C" 354**th **Engineer Construction Battalion, United States Army*** – I guess you heard I made my sergeant's rating. I finally got what I was working for. Boy, it felt awfully good, believe me. It feels funny to hear the fellows calling me Sarge. Tomorrow, I take over the platoon because our platoon sergeant went on his furlough for ten days. Hell, he has only got one more stripe than me, and pretty soon, I'll catch up to him, too. I am going to go

for that Master, believe me. I might as well get all I can get. ... I have seen a lot of baseball (Major League), and last week, I saw the Giants in New York. What is new in Syracuse? Have they opened the town up yet? If I am on that list, I'll be home for about fifteen or maybe twenty. After all eight months in here and not over yet.

Between 11 and 24 July 1951 – I am on maneuvers. What a bastard of a hell hole this is. It's so damn hot during the day, and then at night, you freeze your balls off. If they don't give me a furlough pretty soon, they can stick this army in their ass. Everything we do is outside. Eat, work, shit outside. The tents we are in sleep ten men, and this place looks like tent city. What a hole. I guess it is overseas for sure after this. We will be here for ten weeks. You probably won't be getting much mail from me because we are way back in the woods.... Did you ever picture the end of the world? Well, this is one step lower. I haven't taken a shower in three days, and all the guys are really pissed off.

24 July 1951 – Well, things are really busting out all over around here, and I mean all over. The Second Army just sent an order down for a hundred and eighty-five men for replacements to Korea next month. That is certainly going to put a big hole in our battalion. No s..t, you get an awful feeling when you find out how really close you are getting. In one way we have been pretty lucky being in the States for close to nine months and not overseas yet. Our advanced party left for Indiantown Gap, Penn. today to survey the job. The rest of the company will be up there by the 15th of August. We are going to build a railroad up there. If I don't get called in that overseas draft I'll only be about 200 miles from home.

5 September 1951 – I had to go to Baltimore to pick up a prisoner the other day, and he took up quite a little of my time. I drove up in a jeep, and I took Joe with me. I am going to Washington on the 12th to see the Robinson and Turpin fight. That should be an awful good

one. You pay two dollars, and you see the fight and a picture. About that list, I was on it but got scratched. Why, I don't know. But I sure thanked God for it. I hope we get out of this place soon. It sure is getting damp and cold at night in these tents, and I am dying of a cold now. I might have to go to Louisiana this week to pick up a prisoner. Why don't some of them guys go to Syracuse and get caught? I sure would like that. I saw the Yanks and Washington last Saturday, Lopat won it 4 and 0. It sure is going to be a close race. I hope the Giants win the national race. I hate that Brooklyn. Of course, it doesn't look like my Red Sox are going to do it this year, either.

19 October 1951 – All of the 059 boys (four of us) had to come up here instead of back to Pickett for our refresher course. The school we are going to doesn't graduate until the first week in Feb. 1952 but we are just up here until about the end of November. They just want us to get as much as we can out of it until the order comes. The clearing of port date is still set for December 11, and we don't know where we are going. I just as soon get out of here and go overseas. I am 14 miles from Washington and 40 miles from Baltimore. What a town that Baltimore is. I was up there last weekend, and it is wide open. Baltimore Street has everything: burlesque and a lot of drinking joints ... I have a funny feeling about life now that we might go over. I don't know, I just don't give a s..t, but don't worry, I'll take care of myself ... So, it's Sergeant First Class now. One more, and I'll be a master, so I might as well buck for the other one now... I am going to try and get home before I go overseas.

24 October 1951 – My school consists of both classes and field problems. I take a squad of men out tomorrow to capture a machine gun emplacement at an intersection of two roads. They have it zeroed in so that the platoon can't get by. We have live ammo, and everything is realistic ... There is a WAC [Women's Army Corps] detachment across the street, and I made a few contacts ... I am in the dark about us going overseas because the co. is back at Pickett.

Off to Germany

28 February 1952 – Well, we left on February 21ˢᵗ at 600 pm out of Hampton Roads, VA, and while the first few days were okay, we hit a storm on day three, and I got seasick as all hell. Boy, I never saw such big waves in all of my life. Will finally see land tomorrow after eight days of water. We're supposed to hit the English Channel then. We pick up a pilot to take us the rest of the way because the Channel is still mined and parts of the North Sea. We are supposed to dock in Bremerhaven, Germany on Saturday. Tomorrow, they are collecting all the American money and changing it to script. Then we have to change that into German Marks.

4 March 1952 – Well, we arrived in Germany and boarded trains and rode all night. When we arrived at our destination, what a disappointment. We got on trucks in some jerkwater town – Parsberg – and drove another 20 miles into the woods. This place was a concentration camp before, and what a hell hole. The closest town we can go to is Nuremberg. That's where they held the war trails. Boy, that town must have taken an awful bombing because some of the buildings are still half-standing. We are near a town called Hohenfels and only 35 miles from the Czech Border, a Russian Zone. Look, if anything ever happens to Ma and Pa, don't contact me; go to the Red Cross, they'll take care of everything. If you get some dough in an envelope, just put it in the bank. **Say hello to everyone and I am always constantly thinking of Syracuse. There is no place like it, Arch.**

5 March 1952 – I am glad to hear that Mom is getting used to me being overseas. I am going to Nuremberg for the weekend and Munich next week. Will have to get all of our traveling in now because once our equipment gets here, we will probably be working six days a week. I read in the Stars & Stripes that the Nats are in first place. I hope they hang in there. We belong to the 39ᵗʰ Combat Group now. Our old group, 211ᵗʰ and the 432ⁿᵈ Engineer Brigade, broke away from us over here. They went to France, just outside Paris. They are all Texas

reserves, and they stuck it to us, those bastards. Tell Mom and Pop I am okay.

16 March 1952 – I took over the platoon as of Friday. My job is platoon sergeant, but they sure messed with me over here. The Encom says you have to be S.F.C. for one year before you get Master, so that screwed me right there. I only have six months in grade. I'll get the platoon but no stripes to go with it. Well I read that the Nats took the eastern division crown. Well, I hope they take the championship. We took a walk the other day up on the highest mountain here and listened to the Russian artillery all day. I guess holy hell would break our over here if they decided to do anything. There is still a rumor that we might move to Stuttgart to build a hospital when we get through here. I hope so. I have been living on cigs most of the month, one pack for a bottle of Cognac, one pack for three bottles of beer, and so on. Let me know if the guys have a softball team this year. Boy, I just get to be good and they draft me.

20 March 1952 – This country is all messed up. They sign the treaty the first of April with Germany, and then the occupation is over with, but we still have troops here. Them krauts will probably jack up their prices, but we will stick it to them when they want cigs and coffee. I'm getting ten bucks a carton, and coffee isn't as good as cigs. Thanks for all the sports books you sent me. This one kid from Chicago kept asking me for them all of the time. His brother is a bookie in Chicago. He's a dago like us. It sure means a lot to me when you write back. I really miss home and Mom and Pop. I realize now what Pop and Mom went through to grow us up. It must hurt them something awful to see one of us go all the time. I hope they never touch Junior (*ed. note Tex's younger brother Dom*).

28 March 1952 – I was telling Ma I'll probably need a suitcase to carry the money around with me. Boy, we had a terrific time in Nuremberg. We made ourselves a little connection to do a little

business. Understand? Very good deal and lots of opportunities. Everybody is in business over here. I read where the Nats will play the Knicks. I also read that Rocky is going to fight Robinson. Boy, I wish I could see that. I am going to play a little softball with the battalion team here and try to get back in shape.

1 April 1952 – Well, I'm getting a 15-day furlough starting May the 5th, and we are all going to Rome, with a stop in Switzerland first. We are going to use traveler's checks because of the trouble carrying all of those Liras. We called the American Express Company, and they gave us the value of Lira to American money. It's 700 to one buck. I figured on giving Pop's sister about $50; now I'll probably give her a couple hundred. We had a little excitement the other night. We have a beer house a mile down the road from the battalion, and they found a kid laying near there dead with his head lying in the creek. I had to be the Sgt. of the Guard that night. It was a homicide, and he had a knife right behind his ear. They were holding two guys from my company and took them to Nuremberg to put the lie detector test on them. Boy, what a night that was. After that, you can't trust anyone around here. Tell everyone I wish them a Happy Easter.

7 April 1952 – I read where the Nats are down 2-1. Well, my orders came through and my furlough for May 5th. It will take twelve hours to get to Pescara. On my way, I'll go through Bologna and spend a week in Rome. Gee, I can't wait to see Italy, Arch. I mean, after hearing about it for twenty-three years, I sort of got butterflies, just like before a big basketball game. I am going to coach the battalion softball team and play second or third base. As far as I know, I'll start back for the States sometime in late September.

12 April 1952 – I don't know what happened to my girl, but I guess I'll get a dear John letter any day now. You know, I really liked that girl a lot, and it's just too bad I had to be in this Army. I hope that I am wrong. Well, Arch, we are building some barracks in this hell hole

right now. Our company has 18 to build. I was at the Nuremberg post last weekend for a baseball school, and boy, it was beautiful. Big brick buildings, px, barber shop, mess hall, etc. Boy, no wonder so many guys re-up when they get over here. I read where the Nats are out. I sure hated hearing that. I made second base on the battalion team, and boy, am I out of shape. You know, Arch, if I could have just hit that curve, I could have made the pros easy.

22 April 1952 – Boy, another few weeks, and I'll be in Italy. I just can't wait. I think they might slap nine more months on us, and then you never can tell. Everyone is extended now except us draftees. We got our ribbons issued yesterday, and boy, them guys hate that stuff. Well, Arch, my Master stripes haven't come thru yet, and boy, that burns my ass. Well, Arch, them (St. Louis) Browns really got off to a fast start. Joe's team, Detroit, hasn't done very well. I really needled him. I think I am going out of business, if you know what I mean. Things are getting a little bit too big for me. The money is there, but I don't like the business.

26 April 1952 – According to your letter, I guess that I have a lot of relatives, but like you said, I'll sort of cater to my aunt (Dad's sister) and her children. I'll send a picture of the town if I can with the camera I am bringing. We played two games this week, and I played in only one and went 3 for 4. We are still working as hard as ever rebuilding this dump. Few more reserves are leaving for the States next week. Those lucky guys.

19 May 1952 – I just returned to camp from Italy, and boy, I enjoyed myself very much. I spent a few days in Abbateggio with Pop's sister. That town is really in the mountains. I met our two cousins and all of the other so-called relations. I didn't do too bad with the language. Boy, the whole town turned out when I got there. I went to the town that Pop lived in, and I walked around the town. When I went to Rome, I saw the Pope, and he said a few words to me, and I kissed his

ring. I saw the Colosseum, and it sure was a site. Venice wasn't bad, but too much water. Anytime you want to go someplace, you have to take a boat. I was glad to hear that Vince (Ferretti) made it back home okay. I stopped playing on the baseball team because it was too much. Being a platoon sergeant is a lot. Tell Mom and Dad I'm okay.

5 June 1952 – Well, Arch, the rates are opening up in July, but I have to have a year in the SFC grade before I can make Master. I wanted so much to make it. Our softball team is in first place and I am playing third base and fielding like a demon. I haven't lost the old touch; I am batting cleanup. I am not coaching anymore because it's too much being a platoon sergeant and now they just made me Field 1st Sergeant. Have you heard about the new G.I. Bill? Boy, that will sure come in handy. They figure to pass it very soon.

9 June 1952 EVERYTHING CHANGES IN ONE DAY – Saturday, this kid comes up to me and tells me to get dressed, and we are going to Nuremberg to play with the post-baseball team. I told him I haven't played in three years, but he told me to try anyway. When I get to the clubhouse, there the coach of the team (1st Lt) says *are you Simone?* He had a uniform, glove, bats, everything for me. When I got to the field, I was sure nervous. The field is just as good as any other major league ballpark. The players in the league are all big leaguers or pros. They sent me to play third base, and I was batting second. The game started and the butterflies were sure jumping. I walked my first at-bat and struck out the next time up on a curve ball. You know yourself that if I could have ever hit a curve ball, I'd have been up there in the pros. Nobody ever corrected me. The third time up, I hit one to straightaway center field, that one hopped the center field wall that was 400 feet away. I got as far as third base and almost died of exhaustion. After that smash, I knew I would get a chance. I got another hit in my last at-bat. We play four games a week and practice the other three. All you do is play ball, sleep, and eat. It's really big league, Arch. They have trainers to rub you down. You do nothing

but play ball. No duties at all. Our first baseman played for Baltimore and our shortstop with Buffalo. I have a feeling I can hold my own. As I write this letter, I am waiting for my orders to be cut. I sure hate to leave everyone, but I can't pass up a deal like this. Maybe I'm not too old to play this game after all.

14 June 1952 – My orders came through, and I have a new address in Nuremberg. I've been playing ball all week. The team we are playing today is good. They have a guy from Duke named Frank Dale who they say is better than Curt Simmons. They have an article on him in Sports Magazine. I played second base yesterday and still have that bone bruise on my left hand. My arm is sore from throwing, but hopefully, I can work that back. In my first at-bat I blasted one over the left field wall about 380 feet. What a feeling, Arch, to walk around those bases. Boy, this league is big-time. Crowds and all. I hope I get another one today against this Dale guy. (*ed. note: Francis Dale later became a businessman in Cincinnati and would become one of the owners of the Cincinnati Reds in the 1960's.*)

29th June 1952 – We just got back from a three-game series on the road, and boy, am I bushed. Well, Arch, I got another home run to my credit and a few more hits. Boy, that third base is really a hot corner. My arm is still killing me, but my hands are healing up. Well, Arch, this is a pretty good life, but you're always on the go playing ball. Arch, what do you think about me re-upping for nine months to get rich for five years of reserves? Let me know what you think. Found out that Guy is in France, about 165 miles from Paris. Keep writing Arch, you're the only one that keeps my mail coming and I'll never forget it. It sure means a lot.

7 July 1952 – Just got back from another road trip that we lost, and I only went 4 for 12 and batting .316 currently. Those pitchers keep getting tougher and tougher. I'm back playing third base. I am glad (Joe) Maxim won the fight against Robinson, not only because I had

a little money on him but because he's Italian. I won about half a hundred. The baseball season ends at the end of August so I signed up for the football team so I can stay here. I hope Mom takes that vacation. She needs it. She has a lot of work with all of us men there and nobody to help her. I miss her and Pop both more than you can believe.

14 July 1952 – I haven't come in contact with any big major league players yet but there is a lot of class AAA down to D ball here. I haven't been hitting good lately. I am one for my last twenty and I am sure in a slump. My fielding has been above par, and I found out the coach really needs me now that our shortstop got hurt, and he moved me over there. After baseball, the guys that can play football stay here and then after that is basketball season. I signed up for football and practice starts right after baseball is done. About me re-upping for nine months, I think I'll just come home. I am sort of homesick anyway. The only thing I am worried about is a job, and I don't have one.

22 July 1952 – We are still playing good and we played against a guy named Bob Milliken, who pitched for Montreal a few years ago. He wasn't too fast, and I got a hit off him. Back to third base and batting .282. It's pretty good for me in this league. (*ed. note: Bob Milliken played two years in the major leagues after his military service with Brooklyn in 1953 and 1954. He appeared in one game of the 1953 World Series vs the Yankees.*)

31 July 1952 – We are home this week, but I think I will be out for a while. That cyst I had on my backside is acting up, and I think I am going to the hospital for surgery in a few days. Don't say anything to Mom. I guess my Red Sox will never win a game. My old outfit is moving to Stuttgart next month, and I guess that I'll have to go with them. You see, that's a different post altogether, so I can't play for Nuremberg.

4 August 1952 – Well, Arch, I told you I was going to get that cyst operated on. I got up there and turned chicken shit. I guess I better go

back up there, though, and get it done before it starts to bother me again. I started to play ball again this week. I go to football practice in the morning and baseball in the afternoon. So, you can see that I am keeping myself busy. I should be losing a little bit of weight now. I am going out for quarterback. They run the t-formation, and we open up on September 4th. I was glad to hear that Mom went out to camp. I read about Joey DeJohn and his training camp at Sylvan Beach. And I read about the Basilio vs Davey fight.

25 August 1952 – I still haven't made my mind up about staying in the Army. If I find a good enough job I know I'll stay over here. I know one thing, Arch: I'm not coming home and working in a factory. I can't see grinding away in a factory. I quit playing football. You were right about there being a lot of good players here. The quarterback played three years at Holy Cross and a few pro players and loads of college material. I was just a little out of their class. I am trying to swing a deal where I can get a job in special services with the rank I have. How come DeJohn is fighting Murphy? I was glad to hear that Marciano signed up for the fight.

9 September 1952 – I haven't made my mind up about staying, but it will have to be soon. From the way you sound, I guess Mom and Pop want me to come home. We won the first football game, 14-7. It was a terrific game. I also hope the Chiefs come thru okay. I've been following them thru the season. When is Syracuse University's last game? About them police exams, do you think they might have some more? Are they putting many on the force? Well, it's something to think about. I'll let you know what I am going to do as soon as I know myself!

21 September 1952 – Well, my time is getting short to make up my mind. If I decide to leave, I'll ship out on October 16th. I would hate to come home and have to work in a factory like I told you before. Well, I guess the Yankees clinched the pennant last night and will

probably win the World Series again. The Chiefs didn't do too good in the playoffs. What happened? You know the sports announcer on the army radio over here is from Syracuse. Lt. Tom Decker. I think he was on WSYR. Our football team upset Stuttgart 20-12 last week. This kid from Harvard was really good.

30 September 1952 – Well, I took the step forward today, and I hope I did the right thing. I tried to explain it to Mom, but you might have to explain it to her. I miss you all, including my big brother – that's you. Take care of everything for me.

22 October 1952 – Arch, I hope Mom took it okay. To be truthful, Arch, I am sorry now, but don't ever tell Mom. I want to cry every night, Arch; that's how much it hurts, but I guess I am stuck now. My discharge date is the 30th of September 1953. I hope that things work out for the best. I have been following the Hill team (Syracuse) pretty close. Is Pat Stark the quarterback this year or Stone? Make sure to tell Mom my re-enlistment is only for one year. You know, Pop cried when I left and it was the first time in my life that I ever saw him do that. Please take care of them both until I get back. It might seem funny to you to think that a 24-year-old could feel like I do, but there is no one better in the world than your mother and father, and I sure miss them like hell.

4 November 1952 – Our football season is over with, except for some post-season games. We are going to a city outside of Rome, Italy, to play a game on Thanksgiving. I am not playing but attached to the team. I hope to get assigned to Special Services for good soon. Played basketball earlier today, and next week I start to train the junior Golden Gloves Class. They are the dependents' kids from 6-15 years old. We have a regular boxing card every so often. Hopefully, I get the trainer's job for the boxing team. I bet the farm on the Syracuse vs Holy Cross game last week. Thank God they won with the 13 points.

5 November 1952 – I am waiting up for the election returns. I like Stevenson in a close race myself, but then again, you can never tell. I lost my vote over here, but I'd have voted for Stevenson myself. I saw the Nats are playing. Have they got the same team?

10 November 1952 – To start off with, I made money on Syracuse Football again. I bet them with 6 points (against Penn State). Gee, they knocked off two bowl-bound teams already. My boy Pat Stark must be really making a name for himself. Well, Arch, he went to College, and I didn't. That's the breaks. I am still on Special Duty to the Athletic office and on the football roster. In a few weeks, I'll probably be assigned to the infantry platoon of the detachment, but I am still looking to get assigned to special services. I am pretty sure I will get it. Boy, then it will be a lot easier, that is, working in all of the sports. I'll probably get the job of coaching the American-dependent school kids every day in boxing. Then, I'll get the train-er's job for the regular boxing team. You see, when you get that kind of work, they call it special duty, and you don't have to pull duties, and you do what you want. I hope it all works out. It will make it a lot easier for me over here. Our football team finished 2-5. They sure have some good players over here and rougher than a bastard. Munich was the best team, with a number of pro and college players. I sure saw a lot of Germany traveling with the football team. They cut out post-level basketball, so that's why I am trying to get on the boxing team's roster. Arch, what do you think of getting Mom and Pop a television set for Xmas?

9 December 1952 – I hope Syracuse does okay in the Orange Bowl, but I think Alabama will be too much for them (ed. note: Alabama won 61-6). Our basketball team is 13-1. I am playing out front as a play-maker. I don't get to shoot much except for a few pops. But I have been in the starting lineup and setting up the big boys pretty good and holding my own. My boxing team is shaping up good. We fight our first match on January 3rd

27 December 1952 – Going to Berlin for our first match. My team looks good. I have a heavyweight that really hits hard. I had a pretty good Xmas. I missed Mom and Pop a lot. Hopefully, they are good. I got a letter from Guy Boo and Joe Matera. I guess they like civilian life. Guy said he will be getting married as soon as I get out of the Army.

8 January 1953 – Just got back from Berlin, and my boys did pretty good. It was a four-team meet: Us, Berlin, Frankfurt, and Stuttgart. I had four winners and two losers good for 10 points that tied with Berlin. I won two more exhibitions as well, so I was very pleased with my boys. Berlin was nice, at least the American sector. A lot of nightclubs and historical things to see. We had to go through the Russian zone to get there, and they made us go through after 7:30 pm in the complete dark. We took a tour through the Russian and British sectors and as soon as we got by the checkpoint of the Russian sector, you could see the difference. There are still bricks and everything lying all over the sidewalks, and they haven't even touched the bombed-out buildings. We hardly saw any German people, and the ones we saw looked like hell. The only thing they did was build a big, enormous statue of a Russian soldier holding a kid in his arms and a sword in the other one, smashing a swastika. It is 36 feet tall and weighs over 6 tons. It is in the middle of a cemetery, and it's to honor all the Russian soldiers who died. All in all, it was something to see, and I will never forget it.

15 January 1953 – My boxing team has been keeping me busy. I am sending more money, please take care of it. I was glad to hear that my bonds are coming in okay. I should have something to show for the three years that I have spent in the Army. I read in the *Army Times* that they want to extend the draftees to three years now. I hope to hell that that doesn't include me. Boy, that has me worried.

22 January 1953 – Still counting down the days until my discharge. Been busy with my boxing team. This boy Musser that I have is a

middleweight, and he fights southpaw. The kid hits like a mule with his left hand and is as fast as a welterweight. Maybe I'll be able to get a hold of him when he comes out of the Army. I strained my groin, so I had to stop playing basketball for a bit.

2 February 1953 – I really enjoyed the International Winter Sports games in Garmisch last week. I tried to meet some of the US Team from Saranac Lake but was unsuccessful. My boxing team starts fighting in the elimination tournament. That's to see who represents Europe in the All-Army Finals in the States. My boys won another meet and are getting better and better. We all had to get flu shots this week. It's pretty bad over here right now. I am going to send Mom a 400-day clock, but I am waiting until I find a good one. How are they? They are not having any trouble meeting ends, are they? If they are give them what they need out of my account.

17 February 1953 – I had to stop playing basketball because of my duties with the boxing team. It's just too much. How is mom? You know she writes some terrific letters. You like the picture of my girl over here. What a beautiful blond bombshell.

3 March 1953 – *(ed. note: 4 years later, Tex's daughter Wendy would be born)*. I have been thinking about staying in the Army, not as an enlisted man, but as an officer. My chances would be good because I am a High School graduate, and the engineer's course that I took at Ft. Belvoir would help me very much to get a commission in the engineers. I only have one boxer left in the tournament and he will have trouble making weight.

14 March 1953 – I am now coaching the team that will represent the US in an International meet with eight other countries. They offered me the job, and I took it. It's a lot of work, but I have the best of Europe to work with. My squad will consist of 20 men. I met two big league baseball umpires recently – Bill Summers and Frank Dascoli.

Great guys, and I was in charge of entertaining them. The old baseball team starts soon, and I'll be out there with them. Need to lose some weight. Boy, 185 is too heavy, and it's all in my ass and stomach.

23 March 1953 – Still haven't made up my mind about staying. I never realized it, but you know how much your parents mean to you when you leave home. I read where the Nats lost to the Celtics. That Cousy was hot. Didn't help that Schayes got thrown out. Baseball starts next week, and I am sure that with my extra weight, I will be able to hit the ball farther but won't be able to move much.

2 April 1953 – Well, we are out on the field getting ready for another baseball season. How are the Chiefs looking this year? Is (Ben) Zientara playing with them? He was over here last year. My boxing team fought a German team last week, and we murdered them. We won 9 of the 11 bouts. They are tough but awful weak in the stomach. I guess it's all that German Beer. Sent you more photos. Take a look at that blond. She sure would put hair on your head *(ed. note, Tex's brother was bald)*. Ha Ha! The watches here are cheap. About half the price of the ones in the States. The best watch you can get is an "Omega" or a "Girard-Perregaux."

7 April 1953 – I went out to baseball practice yesterday, and boy, I can't move with all this weight. I hit a few long ones, but the weight has got to go. It would be great if it were all evenly distributed, but it isn't. It must be all this German beer. You never did mention anything about me staying. I don't think now that I made a mistake staying for another year. If I stay, it will be as an officer. What a life they have and no combat. Well, baseball opens up next week, and I like the Cardinals this season. *(ed. note – Cards finished in 4th place, 22 games back of Brooklyn)*. My boxers are doing good. We fight in a tournament next month against the Navy Air Corp. to see who will represent the US in the Amateur Olympics, which includes Italy, France, England, and the rest of them.

19 April 1953 – Have a game today, and I am playing in left field this season, and I like it. It's a lot different after playing the infield all of my life. I think that outfielders should hit a lot better than infielders. There isn't much pressure on them during the course of the game. Still don't know what to do about staying in. I have a very good job here and making good money. I would like to come out of this Army with about five grand. Then I wouldn't have to worry about anything. I can't see grinding away at General Electric for $45 a week when I can make more money here. Of course, you can advise me to go to school on the GI Bill, which is a pretty good deal. I met a nice girl the other day. Her father has really got the paper. He is some big German businessman. She is nineteen and very well-educated and attended a private school which is very expensive around here.

1 May 1953 – Still playing ball but can't lose any weight. I eat like a horse and am always hungry. I will be home whether I stay in the Army or not by September as I will schedule my furlough. Besides, I have to be home for Guy's wedding. I hope I make it. I hate to let him down. We hear the ballgames on the radio every Tuesday and Thursday night at 10:30. That girl I told you about last month gave me the air. That's all there is to it.

13 May 1953 – Play three games on the road this week and I went 6 for 13, and we won all the games. I see where the Chiefs aren't doing so well. I didn't even know that Bobo Holloman pitched for them last year. Was he really that good? Did you get the 400-day clock together okay? Boy, they are beautiful, aren't they? How are the car prices at home? I mean the new ones, especially a Pontiac Catalina.

4 June 1953 – Just got back from a five-day road trip, and the next day, we had to go out to the firing range and stay overnight. We have to qualify every year with the carbine and M-1. I fired expertly. Still playing ball and doing okay. Hitting around .282. It's good for me,

especially in this league. I am still as big as a house. I am always eating. Never stop.

13 June 1953 – How's junior doing? *(ed. note – Tex's brother Dom).* I am sure glad he took my advice and joined the Navy Reserve. Deep down in my heart, I wish they would have let me go to the Navy, but now that it's over with, I guess that it worked out okay. I am still playing leftfield and hitting around .250. Well, the days are getting longer now that I have made my mind up to come home. I was over to personnel to sign my release papers, and they told me my date to go home, which is now August 24th. I will be bringing my buddy Johnny Centrella home for a few days. We have been together for all three years, and I hope he likes Syracuse.

23 June 1953 – I asked Mom if they have a Veterans Hospital in Syracuse *(ed. note – It opened June 14, 1953)* because I will need surgery when I get home on that cyst I have on my backside. *(Ed. note – Sixty-two years later, Tex would spend his final days at that same Hospital).* I am still playing baseball, but can't hit that lousy curveball. I can never get a good piece of it. I either top it or go under it. They sure are having trouble up in Berlin. Them Russians are killing them Krauts off like mad. Just as long as they don't get any crazy ideas. I was up near the Rhine River last week on a field problem, and it was something to see. The bunkers the Germans had were at least eight feet thick. The bridge there is completely underwater. It isn't demolished. The Americans just sunk it! I met Sam Grillo the other day at the baseball game. He was playing ball with the 4th Division team and was surprised to see me. He is a Lt. now and we talked about me going to officer's school when I get back.

15 July 1953 – Looks like the third week in August I will be able to leave. It takes anywhere from ten to twelve days to get to New York from Bremerhaven. If we have good weather, it might be ten days. The Army doesn't have anything faster than that. They are all transports and slow as hell. Boy, it was bad coming over, but the weather

should be better this time of the year. The North Atlantic tosses those little ships all over, and then the North Sea isn't a picnic either. The more I think about it, I believe I am going to take the policeman's exam if they have any openings.

22 July 1953 – Like I told you before, we hold a lot of clinics here in Nuremberg. And while I was here I got to meet a number of pretty important people. Well, this week, Biggie Munn and his entire staff at Michigan were here. I had to show them around and had the opportunity to talk to him all about the game with Syracuse last year. He said he used 61 players that day, and after the game, Roy Simmons (Syracuse Football Coach) told him, "Thanks, Biggie, it could have been worse." *(ed. note – Munn's Michigan team won the 1952 College football championship.)*

27 July 1953 – Less than a month, and I will be out of here. Looks like I have to go to Bremerhaven for three days, and then we ship out. Will have to serve all my time out even after I get back home. I will go to Camp Kilmer in Edison, NJ, for my discharge. Still haven't made my mind up of what I am going to do when I get back home. I guess I'll just shop around a bit. Worse comes to worse I can always go to OCS and back to Army life. That's what worries me; I just don't know what I am going to do. I know one thing for sure: I am not going to work in any factory. If it comes to starving or going to work in a factory, I would pick starving. That's just the way I feel.

6 August 1953 – *(ed. note – The Final Letter)* – Well Arch, this is my last letter. Received my orders yesterday, and on August 14th, I leave this base for Bremerhaven. Remember, don't tell Mom and Pop I am coming home; I want to surprise them. Only you and Marie know. In a few weeks, we will be playing parlays together and going to games. Thank you for getting me through the Army with your letters and reading mine. Like I said before, you're my Big Brother, and I love you very much. *(ed. note – Tex shipped out of Nuremberg on August 14th, 1953. Seven years later, he had a second child, his son John.)*

ABOUT THE AUTHOR

William Humber, C.M., is a member of the Order of Canada and the first historian inducted into Canada's Baseball Hall of Fame. He has authored 13 books, with five on baseball largely focused on the game's history in Canada. As well, he has written on soccer, bicycling, African-Canadian athletes, winter sports, his hometown of Bowmanville, Ontario, and on the topic of urban regeneration. He has been listed in Canada's Who's Who for over 30 years.

A retired Seneca Polytechnic administrator, he was recognized for his work in environmental education, including Canada Mortgage and Housing Corporation's Sustainability Educator of the Year, an Yves Landry Award for sustainability leadership, and by the College and Institutes of Canada for his Green Citizen campaign at Seneca. It was at Seneca he started a late winter course in 1979, "Baseball Spring

Training for Fans" to prepare fans for the season ahead. Though no one ever ran laps, caught flyballs, or struck out, the course had its 46th offering in 2024. Over the years, he organized 25 trips for fans to the Baseball Hall of Fame in Cooperstown, which always included a stop in Syracuse, New York, where the Simone family tended their city's Triple-A baseball team and hosted us with tremendous hospitality. He and his wife Cathie still live in Bowmanville, but the kids, Bradley, Darryl, and Karen, have chosen the attractions of nearby big cities.

EPILOGUE

We hope you enjoyed this book about my dad – Anthony "Tex" Simone. It was a labor of love to work on this with our author, Bill Humber, my sister, Wendy Simone Shoen, and, of course, "The Texan," who provided us with all the material.

While this book chronicles his life and experiences along the way, the most enjoyable memories I have were in the end.

My sister and I promised him we would never send him to a nursing home and took the challenge of caring for him when his Alzheimer's took over his mind.

During one of those days, after getting him ready for another day and helping him get dressed, he looked me in the eyes and told me he loved me and kissed me. He had never done that before, and to this day, I cry unconditionally whenever I think of that.

He prepared us for that moment, and I will forever be grateful. There was no one who could be more loving than my father, no one who could be more respectful of others, no one who could be more hard-working or down to earth. He was a jewel.

He would ask me to bring him to church every day and I would watch him proceed through his ritual of prayers. I sat there each day in the back of the church, wondering what my role was in this. One day, I sat with him instead of sitting in the back of the church. He was so happy and held my hand, and we prayed together; a few days later, he stopped going to church. He accomplished what he wanted. He got me to pray with him. Since that day, I take time to pray, like he did, and I feel his presence.

You're home now, Dad, but your city, your baseball field, your street sign, your kids, grandkids, great-grandchildren, and the many fans and friends you left behind all miss you.

Thank you, Dad, for all you gave me and my children. You built a legacy that includes being Italian, an athlete, a war veteran, and a baseball icon. We know you have finally gone home to that place that transcends all understanding. We'll be together soon to be with you again.

For more stories and pictures please visit www.texsimone.com

www.ingramcontent.com/pod-product-compliance
Lightning Source LLC
Chambersburg PA
CBHW021638120626
46545CB00002B/608